WORD MASTERY
through
DERIVATIVES

Designed for Students of Latin

ELIZABETH HEIMBACH

Bolchazy-Carducci Publishers, Inc.

Mundelein, Illinois USA

Editor: Donald E. Sprague

Contributing Editors: Laurel Draper and Bridget Dean

Design & Layout: Adam Phillip Velez

Cover Illustration: The cover depicts an excerpt from the *Res Gestae Divi Augusti* (*The Accomplishments of the Divine Augustus*), which is inscribed on one of the walls of the Museum of the Ara Pacis in Rome. The Ara Pacis Augustae or Altar of the Augustan Peace in Rome was erected, by decree of the Senate, in the Campus Martius to celebrate the return of Augustus in 13 BCE from his campaigns in Spain and Gaul. The text of Augustus's autobiographical *Res Gestae Divi Augusti* was found inscribed on the Temple of Augustus and Rome in Ankara, Turkey.

Word Mastery through Derivatives
Designed for Students of Latin

Elizabeth Heimbach

Bolchazy-Carducci Publishers, Inc.
1570 Baskin Road
Mundelein, Illinois 60060
www.bolchazy.com

Printed in the United States of America
2017
by United Graphics

ISBN 978-0-86516-853-4

CONTENTS

APPENDICES

PREFACE

I am sure that, like me, most Latin teachers are constantly being told by former students (and even by strangers when they find out that I am a Latin teacher!) that Latin helped enlarge their vocabulary in English. At the same time, I often see students in my current classes who struggle to master every set of new Latin vocabulary words. They have trouble remembering the principal parts of many verbs, the genitives of important nouns. They mix up the meanings of *ad* and *ab* and *ante*. They don't see how *melior* can be related to *bonus*. They need a way to connect Latin words to their English meanings! Fortunately, English derivatives are a great way to provide that connection, and this workbook is especially designed to help students master a variety of useful Latin words by associating them with interesting English derivatives. I hope that it will be a boon to Latin students and their teachers alike!

I am enormously grateful to my editor Don Sprague, whose patience and knowledge are unparalleled. I also thank his colleagues editors Bridget Dean and Laurel Draper for their perspicacious proofing of the text and Adam Velez for his design and layout work. I am indebted to David Perry for his help with macrons, to my eagle-eyed daughter Susan for proofreading the whole manuscript not once but twice, to my husband Jim for solving the endless problems with my computer, and to my daughter Nancy for her cheerful support of the project.

Elizabeth Heimbach
Port Royal, Virginia

INTRODUCTION

Learning Latin vocabulary is hard work. Not only is it necessary to learn the English meaning of many, many new words, but Latin words are really complicated. They add endings! They change form! There is a lot to learn for each noun, pronoun, adjective, and verb! What is a student to do? Give up? Never! The English language itself can save the day.

English helps with learning Latin vocabulary because more than half of the words in English have roots in Latin. Suppose you are trying to learn the Latin word *ambulat*. If you think of the English word "amble," which means "stroll," it will be easy to remember that *ambulat* means "walk." And if you know other English words like "ambulatory" (able to walk) and "somnambulist" (sleepwalker), these additional words will also help you remember the definition of *ambulat*. Of course, if you did not know one of those English words, you could use the Latin root to figure out its meaning. Learning Latin vocabulary is always a great way to increase your English vocabulary!

Using your knowledge of Latin roots to figure out the meaning of an unfamiliar English word can also give you interesting insights. For example, if you think about the English word "preamble," you know that *pre–* means before and that "amble" comes from *ambulat*. Put the two parts of the word together, and clearly a "preamble" is "a preliminary walk, an introduction." Thus, the Preamble of the United States Constitution reminds readers to slow down and pay attention to the ideas that are being introduced because they will be developed later in the document.

Why do so many English words like "preamble" have Latin roots? It might seem logical to suppose that Latin came into English when the Romans conquered Britannia in 43 CE. In fact, Latin died out as a spoken language in Britain after the Romans withdrew in the third century CE, and it was not until the Norman Conquest in 1066 that Latin roots began to be an important element of the English language. The Normans spoke French, a Romance language (one of the European languages with lots of words that come from Latin), so it is thanks to the French-speaking Normans that so many of the words in modern English are derived from Latin.

In this little book you will find chapters with English words that derive from the Latin words for animals, or for colors, or for money, or for numbers. You will also find chapters devoted to vocabulary that is based on Latin words suitable for a holiday like Thanksgiving. Other chapters, however, are designed to help you learn Latin words grouped grammatically. You will find ways to master the nominative and genitive of frequently found nouns, the principal parts of some important Latin verbs, and the meanings of commonly found prepositions. Exercises in each chapter will help you learn both the meanings of the Latin words and some of the English words derived from the Latin.

As a study aid, Appendix A contains a chapter-by-chapter alphabetical list of the derivatives you are expected to learn for a given chapter. (The lists for chapters 1 and 2 present the suffixes and prefixes presented in the chapters rather than English derivatives.) The bolded words are those defined in the chapter essay or presented in exercise I, while the other words are from the other exercises. Appendix B lists all the Latin phrases introduced throughout the workbook.

The English word "derive" has Latin roots: *dē* is a Latin preposition that means "down from"; the Latin *rīvus* (stream or river) gives us *–rive*. The word clearly suggests that languages flow from a spring or source, just like a river. So, let derivatives help you learn your Latin vocabulary, and let the Latin help you expand your understanding of English words! Happy sailing on the river of language!

PART I

Affixes

CHAPTER 1
SUFFIXES

The English words "affix," "suffix," and "prefix" are all derivatives from the Latin perfect passive participle *affixus* from *affingō* meaning "fasten to." An "affix" is one or more sounds or letters occurring as a bound form attached or fastened to the beginning or end of a word or base. A "suffix" is attached to the end of word, while a "prefix" is attached to the beginning of a word. Note the prefixes *ad* in "affix," *sub* in "suffix," and *pre* in "prefix." The first two have undergone assimilation—the *d* and the *b* when sounded alongside the *f* become *f* sounds themselves. An affix can be either a prefix or a suffix!

In both Latin and English, suffixes can be an important element in figuring out the meaning of unfamiliar words. For example, when you know that the ending *–tor* indicates a person who does something, and you know that the Latin verb *imperō* means "command," it is easy to see that an *imperātor* is "a commander." The *–tor* suffix comes into English in words like "aviator" (airman, pilot) and "cantor" (an official in a synagogue or church who sings or chants, or a choir leader in some religions). Interestingly, there is also an outdated suffix in English, *–trix*, which indicates a woman who performs a particular job. Thus, an "executrix" is a woman tasked with settling an estate while an "executor" is a man charged with the same duty. There is even a word for a woman pilot: "aviatrix"!

The Latin suffix *–ōsus* (full of) comes into English as *–ous* or *–ose*. In this way, *perīculōsus* in Latin becomes "perilous" in English, and both words mean "full of danger." Similarly, "lachrymose" (tearful) comes from the Latin word *lacrima* (tear) with *–ose* as the suffix.

Another interesting suffix is the syllable *–esce*. It indicates an action that is beginning and is not yet complete. The connotation of the *–escō* in *adolescō* (to grow up) is clear in both the Latin word *adulescēns* (young man) and the English derivative "adolescent" (teenager).

English words that end in *–ndum* or *–nda* usually imply necessity. These words are derived from a Latin verb form called a gerundive, which is often translated with the words "must be." *Memorāre* in Latin means "remember," and "a memorandum" is "something you must remember." *Agere* in Latin means "do," and "an agenda" in English means "a list of things that must be done."

Like the endings *–ndum* or *–nda*, the suffix *–ure* is derived from a Latin verb form. However, this suffix has taken on a new connotation in English. The Latin ending *–ūrus* indicates something that will happen in the future, something "about to happen." *Scriptūrus*, for example, means "about to write." But English words with the suffix *–ure* do not imply futurity. Instead, *–ure* is simply a noun ending in English; for example, the word "scripture" is a noun meaning "a sacred writing."

Some suffixes, such as *–il*, *–ule*, *–ol*, and *–el*, indicate diminutives in Latin as well as English. For instance, *cōdex* in Latin means "a book made up of wooden tablets tied together," and *cōdicillī* are "small tablets" like the ones that Pliny mentions in his letter about the eruption of Vesuvius. In English "a codicil" is "an additional clause added to a will." Other Latin diminutives do not have English equivalents, but are easy to translate. For example, when Cicero announces the birth of his newborn son in a letter to a friend, it is not hard to translate *filiolus* (little son). And when the poet Catullus calls his book of poems a *libellus*, it is clear that he means he has written "a little book."

In English, suffixes are especially useful in figuring out the part of speech played by a word that you do not recognize. For example, it can be helpful to associate the suffix *–fy* (make) with verbs like "pacify" (make peace). On the other hand, the endings *–ence* and *–ance* (condition of being full) are noun endings, as are *–tion* or *–ation* (act of), *–ment* (state of), and *–ary* or *–arium* (place for). Similarly, you can expect an adjective when you encounter an English word with the suffix *–al*, *–an*, *–ar*, or *–ary* (pertaining to), *–able* or *–ible* (able to be), *–ine* (like, similar to), or *–ate* (possessing). Of course, you have probably noticed that in addition to its role with adjectives, the suffix *–ate* often simply functions as a verb ending. You see *–ate* in English verbs like "frustrate" and "reiterate." Note that the suffix *–ary* also functions as an adjective meaning "pertaining to."

Finally, it can also be useful to know several important suffixes that have come into English from Greek. These include the noun endings *–graphy* (the art of writing) and *–logy* (the science of). When you recognize these suffixes, it is easy to define English words like "cartography" (the art of map making) and "horology" (the science of measuring hours/time, i.e., the study of clock making).

EXERCISES

I. Make a flash card for each of these thirty-three suffixes commonly found in English. Use a different color of ink for each part of speech.

Verb
–esce = begin
–fy = make
–ate = (indicator of a verb)

Noun
–ance, *–ence* = condition of being full
–ary, *–arium* = place for
–ation, *–tion* = act of
–el, *–il*, *–ol*, *–ule* = little
–ment = state of
–ndum, *–nda*, *–nd* = must be
–tor, *–trix* = one who does
–ure = (indicator of a noun)

Adjective
–able, *–ible* = able to be
–al, *–an*, *–ian*, *–ar*, *–ary* = pertaining to
–ate, *–ent* = possessing
–ine, *–ile* = like, similar to
–ose = full of

Greek
–graphy = the art of writing
–logy = the science of

II. Give the English for each Latin word.

1. imperātor, -ōris (m.) _____

2. adulescēns, -entis (m.) _____

3. perīculōsus, -a, -um _____

4. cōdicillī, -ōrum (m. pl.) _____

5. fīliolus, -ī (m.) _____

III. Give the English meaning of the words below.

1. lector _____

2. crescent _____

3. memorandum _____

4. lachrymose _____

5. scripture _____

IV. Match these English suffixes to their meanings.

1. _____ *–fy*   A.   able to be

2. _____ *–arium*   B.   little

3. _____ *–able*   C.   full of

4. _____ *–ation*   D.   like, similar to

5. _____ *–ose*   E.   act of

6. _____ *–ine*   F.   possessing (or indicating a verb)

7. _____ *–ule*   G.   make

8. _____ *–ate*   H.   place for

9. _____ *–nda*   I.   one who

10. _____ *–tor*   J.   must be

V. For each English word below give the meaning of both the Latin root word and the suffix. Then, give the meaning of the word.

e.g.   deify   *deus* (god) + *–fy* (make) = make a god, raise to the condition of a god

1.   clarify   _____

2.   satisfy   _____

3.   credence   _____

4.   repugnance   _____

5.   elocution   _____

6.   malediction   _____

7.   repatriation   _____

8.   armament   _____

9.   dorsal   _____

10.   intractable   _____

11.   sensate   _____

12.   frustrate   _____

13.   aquiline   _____

14.   terrarium   _____

15.   lector   _____

16.   cartography   _____

CHAPTER 2
PREPOSITION AND PREFIX DERIVATIVES

Latin prepositions are an essential part of a Latin student's vocabulary, and a great way to master them is to recognize the Latin prepositions that show up as prefixes in English words. For example, when you know that the "circumference" of a circle is "the distance around its boundary," that "circum-navigate" means "sail around," and that "circumlocution" means "a roundabout way of speaking," it is easy to remember that the Latin preposition *circum* means "around." "Contradict" means "say the opposite," and "a contrarian" is "a person who always disagrees," so it is logical to assume that *contrā* in Latin means "against." Similarly, if you know that the "antebellum" period in American history refers to "the time before the Civil War," and that "antediluvian" means "before the flood" (i.e., before the flood described in Genesis in the story of Noah's ark and, therefore, very old), you know that *ante* in Latin must mean "before." In the same way, knowing that "an adjunct professor" is "a teacher who has been added **to** the staff in a temporary capacity" helps you remember that *ad* in Latin must mean "to" or "toward." Familiar words like "transfer," "translate," and "transportation" are reminders that *trāns*, in Latin, means "across," while "postpone" tells you that *post* means "after." Even words like "ultraviolet" or "infrared" can help you recognize that *ultrā* means "beyond" and *infrā* means "below" when you know that "ultraviolet light" refers to "light waves that are beyond the spectrum visible to humans," and "infrared light" is created by "light waves that are below the visible spectrum."

Some Latin prepositions like *sub* actually have two meanings, and again derivatives can be helpful: you can remember that *sub* means not only "under" but also "at the foot of" if you know that "subterranean" means "under the earth," while "suburbs" are "communities at the edge of a city," not under it. By the same token, if you think of "income" meaning "money coming in" while "incoherent" means "unclear," you will be reminded that while the preposition *in* often means "in" or "into," *in* can also mean "against," and as a prefix *in* can mean "not." Of course, a somewhat different situation occurs with the Latin preposition *ex*. In Latin, *ex* literally means "out of," and the English word "exurb" (a community outside or beyond the outskirts of a city) reflects this. However, *ex* as an English prefix is also used in a less literal way to mean "out-of-office." A former president, for example, can be described as an "ex-president."

Sometimes, a Latin preposition actually takes on a different meaning when it becomes an English prefix. For instance, *ob* in Latin means "on account of," but as an English prefix *ob* means "to, on, over, against." An "oblation," therefore, means "an offering," while an "obstacle" is "something that stands in the way." Furthermore, some Latin prepositions may be a little difficult to spot because they change their spelling when they become English prefixes. *Cum*, which means "with," changes to *com* or *co* when it forms English words like "compare" or "cooperate." In addition, a process called assimilation frequently takes place. When assimilation occurs, the Latin preposition prefix changes its last letter to the first letter of the word to which it is attached. Thus, *ad* becomes *ac* when it becomes part of *cēdere* and creates the Latin verb *accēdere*, the root of the English word "accede," which means "yield (*cēdere*) to (*ad*)."

Finally, it is important to recognize that, in addition to their role as English prefixes, Latin prepositions are also found in many Latin phrases in everyday English. Phrases like *per diem* ("by the day" or "for each day") or *ad nauseam* ("to a sickening degree") will, therefore, reinforce your knowledge of a number of Latin prepositions.

EXERCISES

I. Fill in the blank with the meaning of each English word. Some of the English meanings were discussed above, some may require a dictionary, and some you may know already or can guess.

Latin preposition	English word	Meaning of English
1. *ā, ab* = from, by	abstract	
2. *cum* = with	concede	
3. *dē* = down from	dejected	
4. *sine* = without	sinecure	
5. *prō* = for, on behalf of	proactive	
6. *sub* = under, at the foot of	subtract	
7. *ē, ex* = out of	exurbs	
	exorbitant	
8. *in* = in, into, against	inanimate	
9. *ad* = to, toward	adjunct	
10. *ante* = before	antediluvian	
11. *circum* = around	circumlocution	
12. *contrā* = against	contrarian	
13. *infrā* = below	infrared	
14. *inter* = between, among	interlocutor	
	interregnum	
15. *ob* = on account of	obviate	
16. *post* = after	postprandial	
17. *per* = through, by	peruse	
18. *praeter* = beyond	preternatural	

19. *super* = above   superannuated   _____

20. *trāns* = across   translucent   _____

21. *ultrā* = beyond   ultraviolet   _____

II. Use a dictionary to find the meanings of these phrases.

1. ad nauseam   _____

2. per capita   _____

3. ante bellum   _____

4. ante meridiem (A.M.)   _____

5. post meridiem (P.M.)   _____

6. post scriptum (P.S.)   _____

7. cum laude   _____

8. ex tempore   _____

9. sine die   _____

10. per diem   _____

11. sub poena   _____

III. Match these Latin prepositions to their English meanings.

1. _____ *ā, ab*   A. with

2. _____ *prō*   B. by, from

3. _____ *ē, ex*   C. for, on behalf of

4. _____ *dē*   D. down from, concerning

5. _____ *ad*   E. before

6. _____ *ante*   F. without

7. _____ *cum*   G. out of

8. _____ *trāns*   H. to, toward

9. _____ *per*   I. across

10. _____ *sine*   J. through

IV. Answer briefly. NB: you may need to use a dictionary or an Internet site.

1. The Latin preposition *cum* often changes to *con*, *com*, or *co* when it becomes an English prefix. What does *com* mean when it is the first syllable of the English word "companion"? Since the Latin word *pānis* means "bread," what is the literal meaning of the English word "companion"?

2. While the prefixes *co* and *con* may mean "with," they sometimes simply strengthen or emphasize the root word to which they are attached. Give the meaning of "conservation."

3. Give the meaning of the English word "oblation." What Latin verb is the root of the syllable *–lat*?

4. The Latin preposition *sine* means "without." What does *sine quā nōn* mean literally? What is its common meaning?

V. Choose and circle the best answer from A, B, C, or D.

1. The English words **abstract**, **detract**, **retract**, and **extract** all come from the Latin verb that means

    A. drag   B. touch
    C. pierce   D. cross

2. When the US Senate adjourns without setting a date to return, what Latin phrase describes the situation?

    A. *ex tempore*   B. *post meridiem*
    C. *sine die*   D. *per capita*

3. The English word **circumlocution** means

    A. indirect language   B. eloquence
    C. careful editing   D. brevity

4. A job that requires little or no work can be described as

    A. a contrarian   B. a sinecure
    C. an adjunct   D. an abstraction

5. Many ghost stories involve events that could be described as

    A. antediluvian   B. preternatural
    C. effusive   D. proactive

6. **Inanimate**, **inept**, and **incoherent** all begin with the prefix *in* meaning

   A. not   B. in
   C. into   D. on

7. The Latin phrase *per capita* literally means "by heads." What does the phrase mean more commonly?

   A. of chief importance   B. by percentage
   C. individually   D. economically

8. The English words **deject**, **inject**, and **eject** all derive from the Latin verb that means

   A. hold   B. lie
   C. turn   D. throw

9. Frosted glass is always

   A. unbreakable   B. translucent
   C. polarized   D. clear

10. A *per diem* allowance covers expenditures incurred by the

   A. day   B. week
   C. month   D. year

PART II

Special Topic Derivatives

CHAPTER 3
ANIMAL DERIVATIVES

The Latin word for "animal" is *animal*! The word is related to *anima*, "breath," and, of course, all living creatures breathe. You can easily recognize other related English derivatives of *anima* like "animation" and "inanimate." However, it may be puzzling to see any relationship between *vacca*, the Latin word for "a young cow," and the English word "vaccination" unless you know a little bit about the horrible disease of smallpox. Nowadays, smallpox is something you read about in history books, but in the eighteenth century, smallpox was a terrifying reality. People died regularly from the sickness, or even if they escaped death, the sufferers were left with permanent scarring. There was no known cure or means of prevention. Then, an English country doctor named Edward Jenner observed that women who milked cows seemed to be immune to the scourge. Even when dairymaids were exposed to people with smallpox, they did not get the disease. Jenner discovered that the cows the women were accustomed to milk had blisters caused by another disease called cowpox. Contact with the blisters seemed to protect the dairymaids, so Jenner tried injecting a small amount of the material from the blisters into some of his patients. Afterward, even when those patients were exposed to smallpox, they were never infected! The process of providing immunity to a disease by injecting patients with a weakened strain of the virus causing the illness was called "vaccination" from *vacca* because the cows with cowpox had saved the dairymaids.

You might have read recently about an outbreak of another disease called "avian" flu. As a Latin student you probably also know the phrase *rāra avis* (a rare bird), which is used in English to describe "an unusual person." Both the word "avian" and the phrase *rāra avis* are reminders of the Latin root word *avis, avis* (f.) meaning "bird." The root *avi* shows up in other words like "aviator" (an airplane pilot), "aviation" (airplane flight), and "aviary" (a bird cage). Of course, the similar-sounding English word "apiary" is not derived from *avis*. It comes from *apis*, the Latin word for "bee," and an "apiary" is "a collection of beehives" while an "apiarist" is "a beekeeper."

A Roman used the word *grex, gregis* for "a flock or herd," and *greg* is the root of English words like "segregate," which means "to cut off (from the flock)," and "egregious," "standing out (from the flock) in a negative way." The English word "congregation" suggests "a flock of people who attend the same church," and a minister can be called a *pastor*, which is the Latin word for "shepherd."

Like sheep, *caprī* (goats) are herd animals. Goats are agile and playful. They clamber up and down rocky terrain easily and quickly. A herd of goats often seems to wander erratically. Thus, the English derivative "capricious" means "inconsistent, fickle, mercurial."

Often Latin words for animals give us adjectives ending in the suffix *–ine*. The suffix means "like" or "similar to," so "aquiline" means "like an eagle" and usually describes a person with a big nose like a beak. Of course, it is important to know the genitive of a Latin word like *leō* because the English "leonine" uses the genitive *leōnis* as its base. Similarly, it is important to know that the genitive of the Latin word *bōs* is *bovis*, and the English word "bovine" means "a cow or cow-like."

Sometimes there are words in Latin for animals that do not seem to have any Latin derivatives. For example, there are two words for "pig" in Latin: *porcus* and *sūs*. "Porcine" (pig-like) and "porky" (fat) obviously come from *porcus*, but what about *sūs*? Here, Latin students have an advantage: they can easily hear and see the derivation of the cry of a pig caller, "Suee, suee!"

EXERCISES

I. Fill in the blank with the meaning of each English word. Some of the English meanings were discussed above, some may require a dictionary, and some you may know already or can guess.

	Latin word	English word	Meaning of English
1.	*avis, avis* (f.) = bird	avian	_____
2.	*apis, apis* (f.) = bee	apiary	_____
3.	*passer, passeris* (m.) = sparrow	passerine	_____
4.	*ovis, ovis* (f.) = sheep	ovine	_____
5.	*taurus, -ī* (m.) = bull	taurine	_____
6.	*bōs, bovis* (c.) = cow	bovine	_____
7.	*leō, leōnis* (m.) = lion	leonine	_____
8.	*aquila, -ae* (f.) = eagle	aquiline	_____
9.	*canis, canis* (c.) = dog	canine	_____
10.	*fēlēs, fēlis* (f.) = cat	feline	_____
11.	*vulpēs, vulpis* (f.) = fox	vulpine	_____
12.	*ursus, -ī* (m.) = bear	ursine	_____
13.	*asinus, -ī* (m.) = donkey, ass	asinine	_____
14.	*vacca, -ae* (f.) = heifer, young cow	vaccine	_____
15.	*caper, caprī* (m.) = goat	capricious	_____
16.	*sīmia, -ae* (f.) = monkey	simian	_____
17.	*mūs, mūris* (c.) = mouse	muscle	_____
18.	*columba, -ae* (f.) = dove	columbarium	_____
19.	*pastor, pastōris* (m.) = shepherd	pastor	_____

20. *grex, gregis* (m.) = flock   congregation   _____

                                   aggregate   _____

                                   egregious   _____

                                   segregate   _____

21. *lupus, -ī* (m.) = wolf   lupine   _____

22. *porcus, -ī* (m.) = pig   porcine   _____

II. Choose and circle the best answer from A, B, C, or D.

1. If an author writes that a character in a novel is **passerine**, you understand that this person is unusually

     A.   tall   B.   lazy

     C.   careless and sloppy   D.   quick moving and agile

2. The English words **congregate**, **segregate**, and **egregious** are all derived from the Latin word *grex, gregis* meaning

     A.   flock   B.   wicked

     C.   gate   D.   outstanding

3. You might describe a man with bushy hair and a flowing beard as

     A.   aquiline   B.   leonine

     C.   porcine   D.   capricious

4. *Taurus* and *vacca* are Latin words that refer to

     A.   felines   B.   ovines

     C.   bovines   D.   canines

5. According to Roman legend, Romulus and Remus were cared for by a *lupa*. What kind of an animal was she?

     A.   a fox   B.   a bear

     C.   a wolf   D.   a goat

6. A person who is **vulpine** is

     A.   sly   B.   careless

     C.   rude   D.   angry

7. Complete this analogy: **simian** : monkey :: **taurine** : _____

     A.   cow   B.   bull

     C.   pig   D.   goat

8. If a poem has a **pastoral** setting, it means that the work takes place

    A. in the underworld
    B. in a school
    C. in the countryside
    D. in an airport

9. The constellation called Ursus Minor reminds us of a myth about a small

    A. sheep
    B. pig
    C. goat
    D. bear

10. Lions, tigers, and cheetahs are kinds of

    A. taurines
    B. bovines
    C. canines
    D. felines

III. Answer briefly. NB: You may need to use a dictionary or an Internet site.

1. If an "apiary" is "a collection of beehives," what is an "apiarist"?

   _____

2. Name an island in the Bay of Naples that takes its name from the Latin word for "goat."

   _____

3. In some churches the minister is called the "pastor." Why is the word "congregation" an especially suitable designation for the people who belong to a church if their leader is a shepherd?

   _____

4. In Latin a *columbārium* is "a dove cote, a bird house with many niches in which doves can build their nests." In English the word "columbarium" refers to a structure that has nothing to do with doves. Where would you find a columbarium? What does it hold?

   _____

5. Why would a person flexing her muscles remind someone of a little mouse?

   _____

6. How is avian flu spread?

   _____

7. The English word "canine" usually refers to a dog. Use a dictionary to find another meaning for "canine."

   _____

8. Use a dictionary to find a meaning for "lupine" that a gardener might know.

   _____

9.   What laboratory animals are used in a "murine" study?

_____

10. Name the animals to which these signs of the zodiac refer: Taurus, Capricorn, Leo.

_____

_____

11. Why might a cow be called Bossy?

_____

IV. Match the Latin word with its English meaning.

1.	_____	*leō*	A.	bull
2.	_____	*taurus*	B.	bird
3.	_____	*avis*	C.	cow
4.	_____	*apis*	D.	lion
5.	_____	*lupus*	E.	bee
6.	_____	*vulpēs*	F.	wolf
7.	_____	*caper*	G.	dove
8.	_____	*columba*	H.	fox
9.	_____	*bōs*	I.	cat
10.	_____	*fēlēs*	J.	goat

V. Just for fun.
Translate the sentences below and use a dictionary to define the English derivatives.

1.   Mūs strīdet.   _____

     strident   _____

2.   Lupus ululat.   _____

     ululation   _____

3.   Serpēns sībilat.   _____

     sibilant   _____

CHAPTER 4
COLOR DERIVATIVES

P oets often create images by using words for color just as artists paint pictures on canvas with actual pigments. When Horace describes the *flōs rosae* (flower of the rose) as *purpurea* (purple, dark red), he is helping his readers visualize the flower he is depicting. In addition, Roman readers might well connect the color *purpurea* with an expensive dye imported from Phoenicia (modern Lebanon) known as *Tyrius murex* (Tyrian purple). They would understand that the rose is as rare and valuable as cloth dyed with Tyrian purple, which was so expensive that it was associated with robes worn by royalty.

A number of interesting English words are related to Latin words for other colors. For example, the English word "albino," meaning "a person or animal characterized by a lack of pigmentation," comes from *albus, -a, -um* (white). Of course, if you have read the Harry Potter books, you know that one of the characters is called Albus Dumbledore. It is no surprise that he is an older man with white hair and a white beard. Another derivative of *albus* is "Albion," a nickname for England. "Albion" is a reminder of the bright, white chalk cliffs on England's southern coast. A second Latin word that sometimes means "white" is *candidus, -a, -um*. Thus, a Roman running for political office would wear "a sparkling white robe" called a *toga candida* so that he would stand out in a crowd. Clearly the English word "candidate" (a political contender) is related to this use of *candidus*. In other contexts, however, *candidus* means "dazzling, fair, or beautiful."

Just as there is more than one word for "white" in Latin, there are several words for "black." One word for "black" in Latin is *niger, nigra, nigrum*, and the English derivative "denigrate" means "disparage, defame." Yet another word for "dark" or "black" is *fuscus, -a, -um*, and the English word "obfuscate," which means "make unclear, darken," is a derivative of *fuscus*.

You may have encountered the English word "rubric," which comes from the Latin word *ruber, rubra, rubrum* meaning "red." "Rubrics" are "the directions or procedure required for a particular exercise or test question." The English meaning of the word reflects the fact that medieval manuscripts often used red lettering for headings or the directions needed to conduct a religious service properly. The words in red stood out from the body of the text because they were important. Today rubrics are not written in red, but they still contain vital information, usually about the scoring of a project. Be careful not to confuse *ruber* with *rubus, rubī* (bramble bush)!

Other English words for colors include "cerulean," which means "bright blue" and comes from the Latin word *caeruleus, -a, -um*; "viridian," which means "pale green" and comes from *viridis, -e* (green); and "fulvous," which means "brown or tawny" and comes from *fulvus, -a, -um* (tawny, yellowish-brown). Even in anatomy, there is a Latin color word: *lūteus, -a, -um* means "yellow," and the *corpus lūteum* is a "yellowish structure in an ovary."

EXERCISES

I.

Fill in the blank with the meaning of each English word. Some of the English meanings were discussed above, some may require a dictionary, and some you may know already or can guess.

Latin word	English word	Meaning of English
1. *purpureus, -a, -um* = purple	porphyry	_____
2. *albus, -a, -um* = white	albino	_____
3. *candidus, -a, -um* = dazzling, white	candid	_____
4. *niger, nigra, nigrum* = black	denigrate	_____
5. *fuscus, -a, -um* = dark, black	obfuscate	_____
6. *ruber, rubra, rubrum* = red	rubicund	_____
	rubric	_____
7. *caeruleus, -a, -um* = blue	cerulean	_____
8. *viridis, -e* = green	viridian	_____
9. *lūteus, -a, -um* = yellow	corpus luteum	_____
10. *aureus, -a, -um* = golden	Au	_____
11. *argenteus, -a, -um* = silver	Ag	_____

II.

Match the Latin word with its English meaning.

1. _____ *aureus*	A. silver
2. _____ *albus*	B. gold
3. _____ *ruber*	C. purple
4. _____ *caeruleus*	D. red
5. _____ *lūteus*	E. dark, black
6. _____ *viridis*	F. yellow
7. _____ *fulvus*	G. green
8. _____ *argenteus*	H. tawny, brown
9. _____ *fuscus*	I. white
10. _____ *purpureus*	J. blue

III. Answer briefly. NB: You may need to use a dictionary or an Internet site.

1. Translate the name of the town called Alba Longa. Where was Alba Longa? What was its role in the early history of Rome?

   _____

   _____

2. What color does bronze turn as it ages?

   _____

3. How do you translate the Latin verb *ērubescere*?

   _____

4. Describe the Roman coin called an *aureus*.

   _____

5. What South American country was named for its silver mines?

   _____

6. Name the colors traditionally worn by the four favorite racing teams in Rome.

   _____

7. Find the meanings of *cānus*, *niveus*, *flāvus*, and *rūfus*.

   _____

   _____

IV. Choose and circle the best answer from A, B, C, or D.

1. The English words **rubric** and **rubicund** both come from the Latin word for

   A. red   B. white
   C. blue   D. black

2. On a sunny summer day the *caelum* (sky) is most likely

   A. *viride*   B. *caeruleum*
   C. *fulvum*   D. *nigrum*

3. Albion is a nickname for

   A. France   B. Canada
   C. Australia   D. England

4. The Latin words *fuscus*, *āter*, and *niger* all mean

    A. bright, white
    C. yellow

    B. dark, black
    D. red

5. Expensive purple dye in the ancient world was manufactured in

    A. *Gallia*
    C. *Hispānia*

    B. *Graecia*
    D. *Phoenica*

V. Just for fun.
Find a picture in a coloring book or draw a picture yourself. Color the picture. Add labels in Latin for each color you use.

CHAPTER 5
MONEY DERIVATIVES

If you have studied Roman mythology, you have probably learned the names and realms of the major deities of Mount Olympus, but have you ever heard of a goddess called *Ops*? Who was *Ops*? What was her realm? *Ops* was not an Olympian, but she was a divinity associated with an important aspect of life: money and resources. We see her name in the Latin word *cōpia*, which means "supply or plenty." Our English word "copious" (abundant or plentiful) is a derivative from *cōpia*. It is also interesting that there is a second Latin word connected with *Ops*: *inopia* means "lack."

Long ago, before coins became the usual way of amassing wealth, Rome seems to have had a system of barter for goods and services. *Pecūnia*, the Latin word for "money," is related to the word *pecus*, meaning "flock or herd." Archeologists have found several examples of third-century BCE bars of bronze stamped with images of pigs or cows. These bars are a reminder of this primitive system of barter. Our English words "pecuniary," meaning "having to do with money," and "impecunious," meaning "without money, poor," both come from the Latin word *pecūnia*.

As Rome developed more sophisticated commercial interests, an official mint was established in Rome in the Temple of Juno Moneta on the Capitoline Hill. *Monēta* is the Latin name for the Greek deity Mnemosyne, the mother of the Muses, and our English word "money" comes from Juno's epithet *Monēta*.

The Latin word for "coin" is *nummus*, and we get the English word "numismatics" (the study of coins) from it. One important Roman coin was the *dēnārius*, which was made of silver. The word *dēnārius* is sometimes translated "penny" in English, and that is why you can see ten-penny nails at a hardware store today marked "10d." A laborer in ancient Rome might earn one *dēnārius* for a day's work. The most valuable Roman coin was the *aureus*, which was made of gold. Chemists today abbreviate the element gold as Au.

The front of a coin is called the obverse, while the back is called the reverse. Both of these English words are derived from the Latin verb *vertere* (turn). Roman children played a game called *capita et nāvēs*, which was like our game of heads or tails. You can probably guess that many Roman coins had *capita* (images of the heads of famous people) on the obverse and *nāvēs* (images of ships) on the reverse.

The Romans had problems with inflation from time to time in the same way that modern countries sometimes do. In fact, the English word "inflation" comes from the Latin verb *flō, flāre*, meaning "inflate or blow up." Roman coins were "blown up" by the addition of cheaper metal to the standard precious metals. Thus, the number of coins in circulation increased, but the value of each coin decreased. Devaluing coins by adding a "base" or cheaper metal is called "debasing" the coinage. It is interesting to note that the Latin preposition *dē* (down from, concerning) is the prefix for the English words "decrease," "devalue," and "debase."

Just before Rome fell in the West, people began to use tiny coins of little value that were too small to have an inscription or a picture. They are called *minimissimī*, and they were used by weight, somewhat as modern stores make use of coins in rolls of a set size.

Where did Romans carry their coins? Not in a pocket because Roman clothes did not have pockets. Sometimes, just in their mouths! More often, Romans put their coins in a *marsuppium* (wallet), a *fiscus* (money bag), or a *bursa* (purse). And you probably know that the English word for "an animal like a kangaroo that carries its young in a pouch" is "a marsupial," while "fiscal" means "having to do with finances," and "reimburse" means "pay back."

EXERCISES

I. Fill in the blank with the meaning of each English word. Some of the English meanings were discussed above, some may require a dictionary, and some you may know already or can guess.

Latin word	English word	Meaning of English
1. *bursa, -ae* (f.) = purse	reimburse	_____
	bursar	_____
2. *fiscus, -ī* (m.) = money bag	fiscal	_____
	confiscate	_____
3. *marsuppium, -ī* (n.) = wallet	marsupial	_____
4. *pecūnia, -ae* (f.) = money	pecuniary	_____
	impecunious	_____
5. *nummus, -ī* (m.) = coin	numismatics	_____
6. *aureus, -ī* (m.) = gold coin	Au	_____
7. *dēnārius, -ī* (m.) = Roman coin, a penny	d.	_____
8. *Ops, Opis* (f.) = goddess of wealth	copious	_____
9. *lucrum, -ī* (n.) = gain, profit	lucrative	_____
10. *mūnus, mūneris* (n.) = gift, reward	remuneration	_____
11. *flō, flāre* = blow	inflation	_____
12. *vertō, vertere* = turn	obverse	_____

II.

Answer briefly. NB: You may need to use a dictionary or an Internet site.

1. What is a *cornū cōpia*? Draw a sketch of a *cornū cōpia* in the space below.

_____

_____

2. Consult a myth book to find the story of the goat Amalthea and her magic horns. Briefly retell the myth.

_____

_____

_____

3. Translate the Latin phrase *Salvē lucrum!* Explain why this is a suitable phrase for a Pompeian business-man to have spelled out in a mosaic on his doorstep.

_____

_____

4. When you read about Roman coins, you learned that an *aureus* was "a valuable coin made of gold," and that the abbreviation in chemistry for gold is Au. Find the Latin words for "iron," "lead," and "silver." Then, give the chemical abbreviations that are used for these metals today.

_____

_____

5. Use a dictionary to find the definitions for these additional "money" words: "plutocrat," "bursary," "capital," "credit."

_____

_____

_____

_____

III. Match the derivative with its English meaning.

1.	_____ lucrative	A.	gold
2.	_____ numismatics	B.	plentiful, abundant
3.	_____ reimburse	C.	pay back
4.	_____ remuneration	D.	study of coins
5.	_____ marsupial	E.	poor
6.	_____ fiscal	F.	related to finances
7.	_____ impecunious	G.	financial reward
8.	_____ copious	H.	financial officer of a college
9.	_____ Au	I.	profitable
10.	_____ bursar	J.	mammals that carry their young in a pouch

IV. Choose and circle the best answer from A, B, C, or D.

1. Stockholders would expect a company's **fiscal** report to include information about

    A. financial affairs   B. employee morale
    C. biographies of new board members   D. executive parking spaces

2. Wombats, kangaroos, and opossums are known as marsupials because their offspring

    A. are hatched from eggs   B. are carried in a pouch
    C. stand immediately after birth   D. eat only leaves

3. The English words **reverse**, **obverse**, **invert**, and **diversion** are derived from the Latin verb

    A. *vīvō*   B. *vetō*
    C. *vertō*   D. *veniō*

4. The Roman mint was located in a temple on the Capitoline Hill. To which Roman deity was that temple dedicated?

    A. Mercury   B. Juno
    C. Janus   D. Venus

5. The **bursar** of a college is in charge of the school's

    A. finances   B. athletics
    C. library   D. technology

6. If a county has a **copious** supply of natural resources, its inhabitants are considered

    A. fortunate   B. illustrious
    C. advanced   D. industrialized

7. **Au** in chemistry is an abbreviation for the Latin word for

    A. gold   B. iron
    C. silver   D. lead

8. Which store would be the best place to find a product labelled 10d (10 penny)?

    A. coffee shop   B. candy store
    C. clothing store   D. hardware store

V. Just for fun.

Find images of Roman coins in a book or on the Internet. Sketch the obverse and the reverse of a coin that you find interesting. Be prepared to explain why you find it interesting.

CHAPTER 6
NUMBER DERIVATIVES

Latin is at the root of numerous number words in English. For example, you can see Latin numbers in the names of the months September, October, November, and December. *Septem* in Latin means "seven," *octō* means "eight," *novem* means "nine," and *decem* means "ten." Of course, you know that September is the ninth month in our calendar, not the seventh month. Similarly, October is not the eighth month, and November and December are not the ninth and tenth months. So, are you wondering how those four months got their names? The answer is that in the early days, the calendar year of Rome began in March. That made September the seventh month, October the eighth, and so on. Later, when the calendar was revised to begin in January, some of the old names did not change. Only two months, *Quintīlis*, the fifth month, and *Sextīlis*, the sixth month, were renamed. *Quintīlis* became *Iūlius* to honor Iūlius Caesar, and *Sextīlis* became *Augustus* to honor the emperor Augustus.

Now, let's think about some other English words that are derived from the Latin words for numbers. What one thing do words like "unify," "unite," "uniform," and "unicorn" have in common? They all begin with the prefix *uni*, which comes from *ūnus*, the Latin word for "one."

Even the motto of the United States has the Latin word *ūnum*. If you look carefully at a dollar bill, you will see a banner held in the eagle's claws. It reads, *E Pluribus Unum*. That phrase is usually translated "out of many one." Of course, Latin students know that *pluribus* is the comparative of the adjective *multus* (many, much) so it literally means "more," not "many." It is interesting that the saying *E Pluribus Unum* was associated in Roman times with soup or stew and meant one dish made up of many different ingredients. Some people say that the motto reflects the image of a melting pot since the citizens of our nation come from many different backgrounds. Other people say the motto is a reminder that the United States is one nation, but it is made up of many individual states.

Ūnus is not the only Latin number with lots of English derivatives. For example, "duo" and "duet" in English are both clearly derived from the Latin word *duo* meaning "two," and the word "quintet" is obviously related to *quīnque*, the Latin word for "five." Latin words for numbers are especially important when you are dealing with the metric system. The Latin words *decem* (10), *centum* (100), and *mīlle* (1,000) are used as prefixes for fractional amounts in the metric system. Thus, a "decimeter" is "one tenth of a meter," a "centimeter" is "one hundredth of a meter," and a "millimeter" is "one thousandth of a meter." "Meter" is itself derived from the Latin *metrum*.

Extra-large numbers in English also have Latin roots. For instance, "a septillion" is 1,000,000,000,000,000, 000,000,000 (one thousand followed by seven groups of three zeroes). Similarly, you know the number of zeroes in the number "vigintillion" if you know that the Latin word for "twenty" is *vigintī*.

Numbers like *ūnus, duo, trēs, decem, centum,* and *mīlle* are called cardinal numbers. The word "cardinal" comes from the Latin word *cardō, cardinis* meaning "hinge." If you consider that hinges are an essential part of a door, you can easily see that numbers used for counting and basic arithmetic are also very important. NB:

Important officials in the Roman Catholic Church are called cardinals. Their robes are red so you can see why red birds are known as cardinals.

In addition to cardinal numbers, both Latin and English have ordinal numbers that put things in order. For example, *primus* in Latin means "first," just as "prime" does in English. Latin ordinals are adjectives that agree with the words they modify in gender, number, and case. You probably know that some Roman men were given first names that are ordinal numbers. Does a name like *Quīntus* always mean a man with four older brothers? Of course not! You see the same thing today with modern names when you realize that a person with the name Taylor does not necessarily do very much sewing!

EXERCISES

I. Fill in the blank with the meaning of each English word. Some of the English meanings were discussed above, some may require a dictionary, and some you may know already or can guess.

Latin word	English word	Meaning of English
1. *ūnus* = one	unify	_____
2. *duo* = two	duet	_____
3. *trēs, tria* = three	triad	_____
	trefoil	_____
4. *quattuor* = four	quadruped	_____
	quadrangle	_____
5. *quīnque* = five	quintet	_____
6. *sex* = six	sextant	_____
7. *septem* = seven	septuagenarian	_____
8. *octō* = eight	octagon	_____
9. *novem* = nine	novena	_____
10. *decem* = ten	decimeter	_____
11. *prīmus* = first	prime	_____
12. *secundus* = second	secondary	_____
13. *tertius* = third	tertiary	_____
14. *quārtus* = fourth	quart	_____
15. *quīntus* = fifth	quintuplets	_____
16. *sextus* = sixth	sextuplets	_____
17. *centum* = 100	centennial	_____
18. *mīlle* = 1,000	millipede	_____

II. Translate.

1. e pluribus unum   _____

2. per centum   _____

III. Match the derivative with its English meaning.

1. _____ duet	A.	seventy-year-old person
2. _____ prime	B.	eight-sided figure
3. _____ novena	C.	of first importance
4. _____ quintuplets	D.	musical work for two voices or two instruments
5. _____ octagon	E.	a group of three
6. _____ trefoil	F.	one-hundredth-year celebration
7. _____ septuagenarian	G.	nine days of prayer in some churches
8. _____ unify	H.	five babies born at one time to the same mother
9. _____ triad	I.	make into a single unit
10. _____ centennial	J.	three-leaf plant

IV. Answer briefly. NB: you may need to use a dictionary or an Internet site.

1. How many political leaders joined with Julius Caesar to form the First Triumvirate?

   _____

2. If a "septuagenarian" is seventy years old, how old is an "octogenarian"?

   _____

3. Which insect has more legs: a "millipede" or a "centipede"?

   _____

4. How many points would you expect to find in a figure called a "quincunx"?

   _____

5. Find the definition of "hectare," "kilometer," and "milligram."

   _____

   _____

6. How many carbon atoms are found in "octane," a component of gasoline?

    _____

7. Give the numbers from one to ten in Spanish.

    _____

    _____

8. Give the numbers from one to ten in French.

    _____

    _____

9. Give the numbers from one to ten in Italian.

    _____

    _____

V. Choose and circle the best answer from A, B, C, or D.

1. Quot efficiuntur, si septem adduntur trēs?

    A. quattuor   B. quīnque
    C. novem   D. decem

2. Quotiēs sunt centum dīvīsum per decem?

    A. IV   B. V
    C. IX   D. X

3. Which is larger?

    A. decimeter   B. centimeter
    C. millimeter   D. meter

4. Quot exstant, si ex decem demptī sunt octō?

    A. ūnus   B. duo
    C. trēs   D. quattuor

5. If an event is described as a quadrennial celebration, how often does it occur?

    A. every year   B. every other year
    C. every four years   D. every decade

VI. Just for fun.

1. Create a worksheet for a student who is learning Roman numerals. Ask a series of questions e.g., the student's age, date and year of birth, year of graduation, number of brothers and sisters, etc. Have your friend complete the handout by giving the answers in Roman numerals.

2. The Latin words for numbers are the root for some very interesting words in English. Look up "quarantine" and explain its current meaning and its connection to a Latin number. Explain the meaning of "quintessential." Be sure to make a connection to Thomas Aquinas and his use of Aristotelian thought. What is the "Septuagisma"?

3. The Greek words for numbers also provide the roots for some equally interesting words. Do you suffer from "triskaidekaphobia"? Make sure your answer accounts for its number origins. What is an Enneagram? What contests are part of a pentathlon? What is the connection of "pentathlon" to the Greek?

4. Use the information below to create a poster for your classroom giving important information about the metric system.

5. Use the information below to create a poster for your classroom giving the derivation of the names of large numbers in English. Be sure to give each number in Arabic numerals.

The Metric System

The Greek word *metron* means "measure" and gives us the English words "meter" and "metric." The **Latin** words for 10, 100, and 1,000 are used as prefixes in the metric system for **fractions** while the **Greek** words are used as prefixes for **multiples**.

Latin

10 = *decem* = deci	decimeter = 1/10 of a meter
100 = *centum* = centi	centimeter = 1/100 of a meter
1,000 = *mīlle* = milli	millimeter = 1/1,000 of a meter

Greek

10 = *deka*	dekameter = 10 meters
100 = *hekaton* = hecta	hectare = 10,000 square meters
1,000 = *chilioi* = kilo	kilometer = 1,000 meters = 5/8 of a mile
	kiloliter = 1,000 liters = 264 gallons

Number Names

thousand	10^3	1,000
million	10^6	1,000,000
billion	10^9	1,000,000,000
trillion	10^{12}	1,000,000,000,000
quadrillion	10^{15}	1,000,000,000,000,000
quintillion	10^{18}	1,000,000,000,000,000,000
sextillion	10^{21}	1,000,000,000,000,000,000,000
septillion	10^{24}	1,000,000,000,000,000,000,000,000
octillion	10^{27}	1,000,000,000,000,000,000,000,000,000
nonillion	10^{30}	1,000,000,000,000,000,000,000,000,000,000
decillion	10^{33}	1,000,000,000,000,000,000,000,000,000,000,000
undecillion	10^{36}	1,000,000,000,000,000,000,000,000,000,000,000,000
duodecillion	10^{39}	1,000,000,000,000,000,000,000,000,000,000,000,000,000
tredecillion	10^{42}	1,000,000,000,000,000,000,000,000,000,000,000,000,000,000
quattuordecillion	10^{45}	1,000,000,000,000,000,000,000,000,000,000,000,000,000,000,000
quindecillion	10^{48}	1,000,000,000,000,000,000,000,000,000,000,000,000,000,000,000,000
sexdecillion	10^{51}	1,000,000,000,000,000,000,000,000,000,000,000,000,000,000,000,000,000
septendecillion	10^{54}	1,000,000,000,000,000,000,000,000,000,000,000,000,000,000,000,000,000,000,000
octodecillion	10^{57}	1,000,000,000,000,000,000,000,000,000,000,000,000,000,000,000,000,000,000,000,000,000
novemdecillion	10^{60}	1,000,000,000,000,000,000,000,000,000,000,000,000,000,000,000,000,000,000,000,000,000,000
vigintillion	10^{63}	1,000,000,000,000,000,000,000,000,000,000,000,000,000,000,000,000,000,000,000,000,000,000,000

CHAPTER 7
BODY PARTS DERIVATIVES

The Latin word for "body" is *corpus*, which gives us English derivatives like "corporal" (bodily) or "corpulent" (fat). And, of course, Latin provides the basis for many body part terms that are useful to anyone interested in medicine or biology. Words for bones like the *tibia* and *ulna* are the same in English and Latin; *cerebrum*, the term in English for "the upper part of the human brain," is the actual word for "brain" in Latin. Other structures like the "kneecap" are derived from related Latin words: *patella*, for example means "a little plate," and indeed the *patella* (kneecap) does resemble an upside-down saucer. *Fibula* (brooch or pin) has given its name to a leg bone with the shape of a safety pin. Similarly, one of the chambers of the human heart is the atrium, and *ātrium* is the Latin word for "the formal living room of a Roman house." *Alvus* is a Latin word meaning "womb or uterus" (the latter of which is itself a Latin word), and the diminutive *alveolus* refers to "an air sac found in the lung." *Capillus* means "hair" in Latin, so it is not surprising that small, hair-like blood vessels are called "capillaries." Similarly, the word *cochlea*, which means "snail" in Latin, refers to "a tiny spiral structure in the human ear that transmits sound when it vibrates."

Latin is especially useful when you encounter an English word like "expectorate": *ex* is a Latin preposition meaning "out," and *pectus, pectoris* is a Latin noun meaning "chest," so "expectorate" obviously means "expel something out of one's chest, spit." *Genū* means "knee" in Latin, and *flectō* means "bend," so "genuflect" must mean "to bend one's knee." *Oculus* is the Latin word for "eye," so an "oculist" must be "an eye specialist." *Dē* is a Latin preposition, meaning "down from," and *caput, capitis* means "head" in Latin, so "decapitate" must mean "behead." It also makes sense that "the most important city of a state or country" is its "capital." The English word "capitol" is related to *caput* as well although the connection is a little more distant: the *Capitōlium* in Rome was the temple to Jupiter, the most important god in the Roman pantheon. The *Capitōlium* stood on the Capitoline Hill just as the US Capitol building dominates Capitol Hill in Washington, DC.

It can be confusing to deal with English words for a particular body part that has roots from both Latin and Greek. For example, the word for "foot" in Greek is *pous, podis* and shows up in words like "podiatry"; the word for "foot" in Latin is *pēs, pedis*, and it gives us words like "pedestal" and "pedestrian." The situation is even more confusing for someone who does not realize that the root *ped* (foot) from the Latin *pēs, pedis* is not the same as the root *ped* (child) from the Greek *paidos*. The English words "pediatrician" and "pedagogue" do not have anything to do with feet!

Sound-alike words can be puzzling too: the Latin word *planta* (heel) sounds as though it has something to do with plants, and one definition of *planta* actually is "a green twig." However, Latin students who have read Vergil's description of the messenger god Mercury in the *Aeneid* know that this deity does not have green twigs anywhere. He has wings on his feet! And, you may of heard of such maladies as "plantar arch," "plantar fasciitis," and "plantar warts." Similarly, two look-alike words, *ōs* (mouth) and *os* (bone), are tricky to translate unless you think about derivatives for each word. *Ōs, ōris* gives us "oral," "mouth related or spoken aloud," while *os, ossis* gives us "ossify," "harden, become like bone." In the same way, it can be hard to distinguish between the Latin adjective *lātus, -a, -um* meaning "wide" and the Latin noun *latus, lateris* meaning "side." Here again, derivatives like "latitude" (width) and "lateral" (pertaining to the side) can help you keep the two words straight.

Perhaps the most baffling connection of all is the one between the English term "funny bone" and the Latin word *umerus* (shoulder or upper arm). Here, it is important to know that the letter *h* was sometimes omitted before a vowel at the beginning of a Latin word. Thus, *umerus* can be written *humerus*. A bump to the funny bone may not be humorous, but *humerus* does sound like the English word "humorous."

EXERCISES

I.

Fill in the blank with the meaning of each English word. Some of the English meanings were discussed above, some may require a dictionary, and some you may know already or can guess.

Latin word	English word	Meaning of English
1. *corpus, corporis* (n.) = body	corporal	_____
2. *capillus, -ī* (m.) = hair	capillary	_____
3. *auris, -is* (f.) = ear	aural	_____
4. *supercilium, -ī* (n.) = eyebrow	supercilious	_____
5. *pectus, pectoris* (n.) = chest, heart	expectorate	_____
	pectoral	_____
6. *manus, -ūs* (f.) = hand	manual	_____
7. *genū, -ūs* (n.) = knee	genuflect	_____
8. *dorsum, -ī* (n.) = back	dorsal	_____
9. *venter, ventris* (m.) = belly	ventral	_____
10. *alvus, -ī* (f.) = womb, uterus	alveoli	_____
11. *cor, cordis* (n.) = heart	cordial	_____
12. *oculus, -ī* (m.) = eye	oculist	_____
13. *caput, capitis* (n.) = head	capital	_____
	decapitate	_____
14. *sinus, -ūs* (m.) = bay, curve, fold	sinus	_____
15. *cochlea, -ae* (f.) = snail	cochlear	_____
16. *cerebrum, -ī* (n.) = brain	cerebral	_____

17. *planta, -ae* (f.) = sole of the foot   plantar   _____

18. *os, ossis* (n.) = bone   ossify   _____

19. *ōs, ōris* (n.) = mouth, face   oral   _____

20. *umerus, -ī* (m.) = shoulder   humerus   _____

21. *digitus, -ī* (m.) = finger   digital   _____

22. *pēs, pedis* (m.) = foot   pedestal   _____

23. *latus, lateris* (n.) = side, flank   lateral   _____

24. *sanguis, sanguinis* (m.) = blood   sanguinary   _____

II. Match the Latin word with its English meaning.

1. _____ *digitus*   A. bone
2. _____ *alvus*   B. ear
3. _____ *pectus*   C. finger
4. _____ *manus*   D. womb, uterus
5. _____ *latus*   E. chest, heart
6. _____ *genū*   F. side, flank
7. _____ *dorsum*   G. knee
8. _____ *venter*   H. hand
9. _____ *auris*   I. back
10. _____ *os, ossis*   J. belly

III. Choose and circle the best answer from A, B, C, or D.

1. Someone who is described as **supercilious** is

   A. haughty   B. angry

   C. graceful   D. conscientious

2. **Accord, concord,** and **cordial** all come from the Latin word that means

   A. head   B. heart

   C. belly   D. shoulder

3. **Digit**, **prestidigitation**, and **digital** all come from the Latin word that means

    A. magic   B. technology
    C. hand   D. finger

4. The city of Rome is sometimes called the *Caput Mundī*. This title means the _____ of the world.

    A. temple   B. belly button
    C. head   D. heart

5. An **oral/aural** exercise involves both

    A. sitting and standing   B. speaking and hearing
    C. watching and taking notes   D. singing and marching

6. If you are looking at a portrait of a famous person, where would you see her *oculus*, her *supercilium*, and her *auris*?

    A. *caput*   B. *manus*
    C. *venter*   D. *pēs*

7. **Manual**, **manuscript**, and **manufacture** all derive from the Latin word for

    A. writing   B. work
    C. hand   D. factory

8. Where is a dolphin's **dorsal** fin?

    A. on its belly   B. on its back
    C. beneath its tail   D. under its mouth

9. Where would you be likely to see someone **genuflect**?

    A. in a restaurant   B. in a theater
    C. in a church   D. in an arena

10. Where would a patient develop **plantar** warts?

    A. on the feet   B. on the hands
    C. on the arms   D. on the legs

IV. Answer briefly. NB: You may need to use your Latin textbook, a dictionary, or an Internet site.

1. How can you tell the difference between the Latin word for "bone" and the Latin word for "mouth"? How can you tell the difference between the Latin word for "wide" and the Latin word for "side"?

   _____

   _____

2. "Sanguinary," a derivative of *sanguis* (blood), means "bloody." What does "sanguine" mean?

   _____

   _____

3. Use the words "Capitol" and "capital" in sentences that show you understand the distinction between the two words.

   _____

   _____

   _____

   _____

4. The Latin word *sinus* can mean "a fold in a garment like a toga." It can also mean "a person's lap or bosom." In addition, *sinus* is used in Latin to mean "a bay or gulf." What do all these meanings have in common? What does "sinus" mean in English?

   _____

   _____

5. *Cochlea* means "snail" in Latin. Describe the structure in a human ear called the "cochlea."

   _____

   _____

6. *Digitus* in Latin means "finger." How do you translate the phrase *digitus pedis*?

   _____

7. When someone is asked to "endorse" a check, where should the check be signed?

   _____

8. *Lūmen, lūminis* (n.) is the Latin word for "light," but in the plural *lūmina* can have another meaning. Check a dictionary and give this meaning.

   _____

V. Just for fun.

1. Find an English derivative from each of these Greek words: *kardia* (heart), *ophthalmos* (eye), *pous, podos* (foot), *osteon* (bone), *pneumonas* (lung).

   _____

   _____

2. Make a drawing or find a large photograph of your favorite athlete, singer, or movie star. Label the image with the Latin words for parts of the body.

CHAPTER 8
POLITICAL DERIVATIVES

A surprising number of modern political terms are derived from Latin. Some, like "senator," are identical in Latin and in English. Many others have Latin roots. This verbal connection between ancient Rome and modern American politics is probably a result of the fact that almost all the men who were responsible for crafting the United States Constitution had received a classical education. Delegates to the Constitutional Convention like James Madison and Alexander Hamilton learned Latin at an early age and knew a lot about Roman literature, history, and government.

Sometimes English and Latin words are exactly the same but have somewhat different meanings. *Vetō*, for example, is a verb in Latin. It means "I forbid" and reflects the power of an executive official called a consul who could countermand any ordinance proposed by a colleague. In English, "veto" can be a noun, and it refers to "the power of a president or a governor to prevent a bill passed by the legislature from becoming law."

Both "senate" and "senator" come from the Latin word *senex* (old man). To a Roman, *senātus* meant a council of elders, and a *senātor* was a member of that council, who listened to speeches and gave advice on important issues like declaring war. Roman senators were not elected. They owed their membership to their upper-class status. They served for life (or until they did something disgraceful). In our system of government, on the other hand, senators serve for a six-year term, and they do more than advise: they create laws!

Other political offices in Rome were elected, and aspiring politicians who wanted to stand out in a crowd of potential voters wore a special toga called a *toga candida*. The word *candida* is obviously the root of our English word "candidate." The *toga candida* was dazzling white, and it made a candidate highly visible. Then as now, candidates wanted to be seen by as many people as possible. The English word "ambition," often ascribed to political types, actually comes from the Latin *ambi* (around) plus *itiō* (going) because Roman candidates walked around meeting people in public places like the Forum, where they could be seen and heard by voters.

The Latin word *vōtum* means "vow or wish," and for much of Roman history, the *cīvēs* (citizens) voted directly. They assembled on the Campus Martius, an open area in Rome that was also used for military maneuvers. Although women could be citizens, only men could vote, and neither slaves nor nonresident aliens had a voice. When citizens assembled to vote, they were arrayed in armor and carried their weapons and shields. They indicated their will by banging on their shields. That noise (*fragor*) from under (*sub*) the shields gives us the English word "suffrage," which means "the right to vote." When modern voters in the United States elect the governor of their state today, they do not bang on their shields, but they do use a word with a Latin root to describe the election. "Gubernatorial" in English means "related to a governor." In Latin *gubernātor* means "the pilot of a ship." We can think of our states as ships in need of expert direction provided by skilled pilots. It is interesting that the metaphor "ship of state" appears in both ancient Greek and Roman literature.

Sometimes a modern politician wins an election by a huge margin, and commentators say that the winner has a "mandate." In Latin the verb *mandō* means "command," so it is easy to see that the two words are related. According to *Webster's College Dictionary*, the winner of such an election has received "a command or authorization to act in a particular way given by the electorate to its representative."

Even the English word "election" comes from Latin. You probably know the Latin verb *legō, legere, lēgī, lēctum*, which means "choose, select" as well as "read." Citizens in a democracy are expected to select their representatives. Of course, in addition to electing public officials, voters today often vote on important issues like school bonds. "An issue that requires approval from everyone" is called a "referendum." You can see that this word is derived from the irregular Latin verb *referō, referre, rettulī, relātum* (carry back), and indeed a referendum brings a decision back to the voters.

EXERCISES

I. Fill in the blank with the meaning of each English word. Some of the English meanings were discussed above, some may require a dictionary, and some you may know already or can guess.

Latin word	English word	Meaning of English
1. *vetō, -āre, -uī, -itum* = forbid	veto	_____
2. *senex, senis* (m.) = old man	senate	_____
	senator	_____
3. *candidus, -a, -um* = dazzling white	candidate	_____
4. *suffrāgium, -ī* (n.) = noise of shield banging	suffrage	_____
5. *ambitiō, -ōnis* (f.) = going around	ambition	_____
6. *cīvis, cīvis* (c.) = citizen	citizen	_____
7. *vōtum, -ī* (n.) = will, vow	vote	_____
8. *gubernātor, -ōris* (m.) = pilot of a ship	gubernatorial	_____
9. *mandō* (1) = command	mandate	_____
10. *legō, -ere, lēgī, lēctum* = choose	election	_____
11. *referō, referre, rettulī, relātum* = bring back	referendum	_____

12. *praesideō, -ēre, -sēdī* = sit in front   president   _____

13. *rēs pūblica* = public business   republic   _____

                       Republican   _____

14. *demos* = people (Greek)   Democrat   _____

15. *servō* (1) = keep, guard, save   conservative   _____

16. *līber, lībera, līberum* = free   liberal   _____

                       liberty   _____

17. *lēx, lēgis* (f.) = law   legal   _____

18. *rādix, rādīcis* (f.) = root   radical   _____

19. *augur, auguris* (c.) = seer, soothsayer   inaugurate   _____

20. *fascis, fascis* (m.) = sticks and ax carried by lictors   fascism   _____

II. Match the Latin word with its English meaning.

1. _____   *līber, lībera, līberum*   A.   old man

2. _____   *senex*   B.   I save, guard, keep

3. _____   *vetō*   C.   pilot of a ship

4. _____   *vōtum*   D.   free

5. _____   *cīvis*   E.   I forbid

6. _____   *mandō*   F.   I carry back

7. _____   *servō*   G.   will, wish, vow

8. _____   *referō*   H.   I command

9. _____   *legō*   I.   I choose, select, read

10. _____   *gubernātor*   J.   citizen

III.

Answer briefly. NB: You may need to use a dictionary or an Internet site; for question 3 you may need a Latin grammar book!

1. Explain the comparison between the governor of a state and the pilot of a ship.

   _____

   _____

2. Find the Greek root of the English word "ballot."

   _____

3. What is the grammatical term for a verb form like *referendum*? What are some other English words that end in *–ndum* or *–nda*? Hint: What do you call a list of items that must be dealt with at a meeting? a list of things that you must remember?

   _____

   _____

4. The Latin phrase *rēs pūblica* means "public affairs or public business." What period of Roman history is called the Republic? For what Latin words does the abbreviation S.P.Q.R. stand? What do the words mean?

   _____

   _____

5. What was the role of a "tribune" in the government of Rome? Why would "Tribune" be an appropriate name for a newspaper?

   _____

   _____

6. Find information about the role of a *lictor* in ancient Rome. Then, find an image of *fascēs*. What do the sticks represent? The ax? Now, find an image of the Lincoln Memorial in Washington, DC. Where do you see a carving of *fascēs*?

   _____

   _____

IV.

Choose and circle the best answer from A, B, C, or D.

1. The English words **sedentary**, **sedate**, and **president** are all derived from the Latin verb that means

   A. select   B. reside

   C. sit   D. pronounce

2. **Senile** and **senescent** derive from the Latin word

   A. *senex*   B. *sensus*
   C. *sentiō*   D. *sēmoveō*

3. Based on your knowledge of its Latin root, what does the English word **mandate** mean?

   A. a mission   B. an announcement
   C. a directive   D. a symbol

4. The Latin phrase that means "unwritten law," sometimes called "common law," is

   A. *lex non visa*   B. *lex non scripta*
   C. *lex incognita*   D. *lex antiqua*

5. **Legible**, **lectern**, **legend**, and **election** are derivatives of the Latin word

   A. *lēniō*   B. *levō*
   C. *legō*   D. *lēgātiō*

6. **Radical** and **eradicate** are derivatives of the Latin word for

   A. root   B. branch
   C. twig   D. trunk

V. Just for fun.
Read these political notices from the walls of buildings in Pompeii. Do you think that these slogans were posted by supporters of the candidate Vatia, or by his enemies? Explain your answer.

1. *Vatiam aed. rogant . . . dormientes universi.* (C.I.L.IV:575)
   NB: *aed = aedilem* = official in charge of public buildings and entertainment.

2. *Vatiam aed. furunculi rog(ant).* (C.I.L.IV:576)

3. *M. Cerrinium Vatiam aed. ovf seribibi universi rogant.* (C.I.L.IV:581)
   [NB: *ovf = oro vos faciatis*]

_____

_____

_____

CHAPTER 9
TIME DERIVATIVES

Latin sayings like *tempus fugit* (time flies), *carpe diem* (seize the day), *mox nox* (soon it will be night), or the poet Horace's famous lament, "*Eheu, fugācēs . . . lābuntur annī*" (the fleeting years slip by) all remind us of the Romans' concern with the passage of time.

In the ancient world, *sōlāria* (sundials) were familiar devices for measuring time. Some people might also have seen a *clepsydra* (an apparatus that used water flowing between two containers) in a court of law. Surprisingly, however, the idea of a sixty-minute hour all year round is a modern one. An *hōra* (hour) varied in length depending on the time of year. It simply represented one-twelfth of the hours of daylight on a given *diēs* (day). Thus, in late December an hour was about forty-five minutes long while in June an hour was closer to eighty minutes. An interesting English derivative from *hōra* is "horology" (the study of clocks).

The Romans referred to the hour that falls in the middle of the *diēs* as *merīdiēs* (noon). The familiar abbreviations A.M. and P.M. remind us today of the Latin phrases *ante merīdiem* (before noon) and *post merīdiem* (after noon). The English word "diary" (a daily journal) is derived from *diēs*, as is the word "circadian," which refers to "the natural rhythms of the human body over a twenty-four-hour period."

Certain days of each *mensis* (month) in the *annus* (year) had specific names. You have probably heard of the *Īdūs* (Ides) and know that they fell on the thirteenth or fifteenth of the month. The first day of every month was called the *kalendae* (kalends), and that is the root of the English word "calendar." It is interesting that *kalendae* is one of the few words in Latin that is spelled with the letter *k*.

The hours of darkness or *nox* (night) were divided into segments of four hours each. Each segment was called a *vigilia* (watch). The English word "vigilant" meaning "watchful" comes from *vigilia*. An interesting English word that comes from *nox* is a term we use for the change of seasons. An equinox, when the hours of daylight and the hours of darkness are *aequus* (equal) occurs twice a year, once in the spring ("Spring or Vernal Equinox," around March 20) and once in the fall ("Autumnal Equinox," around September 23). The shortest day of the year is the "Winter Solstice" (around December 22), while the longest day of the year is the "Summer Solstice" (around June 21). The word "solstice" comes from *sōl* (sun), and the syllable *–sti* is a variant of the Latin verb *stō, stāre* (stand). Thus, the word "solstice" evokes a moment of stasis before the sun continues on its journey, bringing the change of seasons.

The seasons themselves give us words. "Vernal" (spring-like) comes from *vēr* (spring) and "autumnal" (belonging to fall) from *autumnus* (fall). *Aestās* (summer) is the root of the English word "estivate," which means "to spend the summer in a torpid state." Just as some animals escape winter cold through hibernation, others, like toads, seek to avoid summer heat by burrowing underground and lying dormant. Be careful not to confuse *aestās* (summer) with *aetās* (age). If you see the abbreviation *aet.* (aged) in an obituary, you will remember that an announcement of someone's death is more likely to mention age than summer.

The names of the twelve months we find in a modern calendar have all come down to us from ancient Rome. The earliest Roman calendar was based on the phases of the moon, but by the first century BCE, this lunar calendar no longer tracked with the seasons, and Julius Caesar employed Egyptian astronomers to create a new calendar. The last year of the old calendar, 46 BCE, had 445 days and was called the "Last Year of Confusion" (*Annus Confūsiōnis*). In the new calendar the month known as *Quintīlis* was renamed *Iūlius* in Caesar's honor; we still call it July. Caesar's successor, the emperor Augustus, later renamed *Sextīlis* in his own honor and gave it an extra day. The so-called Julian calendar was revised at the direction of Pope Gregory in the sixteenth century, and we still use it today.

Until 153 BCE, the Roman year began in March, and therefore, September was in fact the seventh month, October the eighth, November the ninth, and December the tenth. This accounts for the numbers *septem*, *octō*, *novem*, and *decem* in the names of these months. When the calendar was revised, January became the first month instead of March. The name January was derived from *Iānus*, the two-headed god of doorways, who is a fitting deity for the end of one year and the beginning of another. March is derived from *Martius*, the Roman god of war, while May is named for *Māia*, the mother of the god Mercury. *Iūnō*, the queen of the gods and patron of marriage, gave her name to June.

Two months do not owe their names to either humans or gods. April is related to *aperīre* that means "open," and certainly many flowers blossom and open in April. February is derived from the Latin word *febris* that means "fever." And given the prevalence of illness in February, the name makes sense! The English word "febrile" (feverish) is another derivative of *febris*. It is interesting that the letter *b* in Latin becomes a *v* in English, e.g., "fever." People pronounce both *b* and *v* with their mouths in similar positions.

EXERCISES

I. Fill in the blank with the meaning of each English word. Some of the English meanings were discussed above, some may require a dictionary, and some you may know already or can guess.

Latin word	English word	Meaning of English
1. *tempus, temporis* (n.) = time	contemporary	_____
2. *annus, -ī* (m.) = year	annual	_____
	biennial	_____
	centennial	_____
	millennial	_____
	perennial	_____
3. *mensis, mensis* (f.) = month	mensal	_____
4. *diēs, -ēī* (m.) = day	circadian	_____
5. *hōra, -ae* (f.) = hour	horology	_____

6. *vigilia, -ae* (f.) = watch, ¼ of the night   vigilant   _____

7. *aetās, aetātis* (f.) = age   aet.   _____

8. *saeculum, -ī* (n.) = age, century   secular   _____

9. *aestās, aestātis* (f.) = summer   estivate   _____

10. *hīberna, -ōrum* (n. pl.) = winter camp   hibernate   _____

11. *autumnus, -ī* (m.) = fall   autumnal   _____

12. *vēr, vēris* (n.) = spring   vernal   _____

13. *sōl, sōlis* (m.) = sun   solstice   _____

14. *nox, noctis* (f.) = night   equinox   _____

15. *kalendae, -ārum* (f. pl.) = first day of the month   calendar   _____

16. *aeternus, -a, -um* = eternal, everlasting   sempiternal   _____

17. *merīdiēs, -ēī* (m.) = noon   Ante Meridiem   _____

   Post Meridiem   _____

18. *febris, febris* (f.) = fever   febrile   _____

II. Translate.

1. anno domini (A.D.)   _____

2. dies irae   _____

3. tempus fugit   _____

4. carpe diem   _____

5. mox nox   _____

III. Match the Latin word with its English meaning.

1. _____ *diēs*   A. eternal
2. _____ *hōra*   B. age
3. _____ *mensis*   C. spring
4. _____ *annus*   D. century
5. _____ *aetās*   E. day
6. _____ *aestās*   F. hour
7. _____ *vigilia*   G. month
8. _____ *vēr*   H. year
9. _____ *aeternus*   I. watch
10. _____ *saeculum*   J. summer

IV. Answer briefly. NB: You may need to use a dictionary or an Internet site.

1. Why did Julius Caesar feel it was necessary to revise the calendar that was then in use in Rome? When did the revision take place? What was the new calendar called? When was the Gregorian calendar first used in Western Europe? When was it used in England?

_____

_____

_____

2. In what section of a newspaper would you see the abbreviation *aet.*? What does *aet.* stand for?

_____

3. Find the definition of the English word "secular." Then, explain how it is related to the Latin word *saeculum*. Find the phrase *Novus Ordo Seclorum* on a dollar bill. Translate the phrase.

_____

_____

4. Define the English word "vigilante." With what periods of American history is the term "vigilante" especially associated?

_____

5. Why do the dates for each solstice and equinox vary from year to year?

   _____

6. Find out more about the Roman god Janus. What does Janus preside over? Why is it appropriate that the month of January is derived from his name? How is Janus depicted on coins? Describe the appearance of temples of Janus in Rome. According to Roman tradition, when were the gates of the Temple of Janus closed?

   _____

   _____

   _____

   _____

   _____

V. Choose and circle the best answer from A, B, C, or D.

1. The English words **perennial**, **biennial**, and **centennial** are derived from the Latin word for

    A. century   B. year
    C. month   D. age

2. Traveling from one time zone to another can upset a person's _____ rhythms.

    A. secular   B. mensal
    C. annual   D. circadian

3. The Autumnal Equinox, which marks the first day of autumn, occurs in

    A. August   B. September
    C. October   D. November

4. The first day of each month in the Roman calendar was known as the

    A. *kalendae*   B. *nōnae*
    C. *īdūs*   D. *prīdiē*

5. Animals such as toads burrow underground in summer to escape the hot weather. This is called

    A. inhumation   B. hibernation
    C. estivation   D. renovation

VI. Just for fun.

1. Find an image of a *clepsydra* (Roman water clock). Make a simple model of this kind of ancient time piece using two small plastic containers. Drill a small hole in the bottom of one container and fill it with water. Note the amount of time it takes for the water to drip from one container to the other.

2. Find an image of a sundial. Make a small model of a sundial using poster board and a dowel for the gnomon.

3. The months of January, March, May, and June all come from the names of Roman deities. Create a poster with images of Janus, Mars, Maia, and Juno that you have printed or drawn. Under each picture write a brief description of the deity's realm.

CHAPTER 10
MYTHOLOGY DERIVATIVES

Myths are filled with amazing adventures, marvelous metamorphoses, and supernatural beings endowed with extraordinary powers. No wonder they have fascinated generations of listeners, readers, artists, and authors! If you have studied Homer's *Odyssey*, or read the Percy Jackson novels, or if you have watched the Disney cartoon *Hercules*, you probably recognize the names, realms, and symbols of most of the Olympian deities in Greek. And when you know, for example, that Aphrodite is the Greek goddess of love and beauty, you can easily see the root of the English word "aphrodisiac" (love potion). You have probably also noted that in some depictions of Aphrodite, the goddess is accompanied by a chubby, winged cherub. This is Aphrodite's son Eros, and his name is the root of the English word "erotic" (sensual).

It is not surprising that many of the Greek deities have Roman counterparts. Thus, there is a Latin equivalent of Eros, a deity called Cupid whose name is connected to the Latin noun *cupiditās* (longing, greed), the verb *cupiō* (desire, long for), and the adjective *cupidus* (desirous, eager). The word "cupidity," which means "greed," is an English derivative.

Other derivatives from the names of Roman gods are also easy to spot. For example, the lame craftsman god Vulcan was the benefactor of artisans and blacksmiths who use fire. The English words "volcano" (a vent in the earth's crust through which molten lava and ash are expelled) and "vulcanize" (to treat rubber with heat) are reminders of this ancient god. Similarly, the English word "mercurial" (volatile, fickle) makes sense when you know that Mercury, the counterpart of the Greek Hermes, was the messenger god, the patron of merchants and thieves. The wings on his feet enabled him to fly swiftly down to earth from the realm of the gods on Mount Olympus. Mercury also led the spirits of the dead to the Underworld. No wonder the element mercury, which is a fast-flowing liquid metal, bears his name! It is fitting that another name for mercury in English is quicksilver and that a volatile character in Shakespeare's *Romeo and Juliet* bears the name Mercutio.

It is easy to see the connection between the names of mythological deities like Cupid or Mercury and English words like "cupidity" or "mercurial," but sometimes the link is less obvious. For instance, "jovial" (jolly, good humored) is derived from Jupiter, the king of the Olympians. *Jovis* is the genitive of *Iuppiter*, and medieval astrologers considered that people born under the sign of the planet Jupiter were good humored. Just as "jovial" comes from the genitive of *Iuppiter*, "venereal" (sexually transmitted) comes from *Veneris*, the genitive of *Venus*, who is the goddess of love.

Besides the English words directly derived from the names of ancient gods and goddesses there are a number of interesting words associated with mythology such as "nectar" and "ambrosia." "Nectar" was the drink of the gods and "ambrosia" was the food of the gods. Today, however, "ambrosia" can be any delectable food or a special dessert made of oranges and coconut, while "nectar" means a delicious drink or undiluted fruit juice. Similarly, the word "lyre" once meant the small harp-like musical instrument especially associated with Apollo. Today, the English derivative "lyric" refers to the "words of a song or a genre of poetry filled with personal emotion." Furthermore, "the major gods as a group" are known as a "pantheon," and pantheon, from the Greek *pan* meaning "all" and *theos* meaning "god," is also used today to mean "a realm of gods and heroes." The Baseball Hall of Fame, for example, might be described as a pantheon.

Even the rivers of the Underworld, Pluto's realm, have given us new words. The words "lethal" meaning "deadly" and "lethargic" meaning "sluggish" both come from the river Lethe. Romans believed that the waters of the Lethe made one forgetful. "Stygian" meaning "dark" comes from the river Styx (whose genitive is *Stygis*). Some of the gods' symbols have also taken on new meaning. For instance, the shield of Minerva (Athena), known as the "aegis," has come to mean "sponsorship, protection, or support." The cornucopia (horn of plenty), once the sign of Ceres, goddess of agriculture, is used today as a symbol of abundance. Aesculapius, the god of medicine, has given his rod with a single snake, associated by the ancients with healing, as a symbol of medicine. The caduceus, Mercury's winged messenger staff, has also become a recognized symbol of medicine because of its two snakes and the story that Mercury reconciled the two snakes that were attacking one another.

EXERCISES

NB: Before you complete exercises I–V, you may want to review the names of the deities in Greek and in Latin. The exercises marked with asterisks that follow exercise V are intended to help with this review.

I. Fill in the blank with the meaning of each English word. Some of the English meanings were discussed above, some may require a dictionary, and some you may know already or can guess:

Deity	Realm	English Word	Meaning of English
1. Aphrodite	love, beauty	aphrodisiac	_____
2. Ceres	agriculture	cereal	_____
3. Cupid	passion, desire	cupidity	_____
4. Eros	passion, desire	erotic	_____
5. Juno	queen of the gods	Junoesque	_____
6. Jupiter, Jovis	king of the gods	jovial	_____
7. Mars, Martis	war	martial	_____
8. Mercury	messenger	mercurial	_____
9. Venus, Veneris	love, beauty	venereal	_____
10. Vulcan	craftsmen	vulcanize	_____

II. Fill in the blanks using the word bank.

aegis   ambrosia   caduceus   cornucopia
lyrics   nectar   pantheon   trident

1. Undiluted fruit juice is called _____.

2. Oscar winners could be said to have joined the _____ of outstanding entertainers.

3. The fruit spilled out of the _____ that served as a centerpiece on the banquet table.

4. A fisherman in the Mediterranean might use a _____ to spear his catch.

5. The medical arts building was easy to identify because of the _____ on the sign.

6. The young intern was grateful to have begun work under the _____ of a kind mentor.

7. Do you know the _____ to this song?

III. Use a Latin grammar book, a mythology handbook, or the Internet to answer these questions.

1. Which planets in our solar system are named for ancient deities? List the characteristics traditionally associated with each divinity and explain where possible why those characteristics inspired astronomers to assign that name to a particular planet. NB: Saturn was the Roman name for the Greek god Cronus, who belonged to an earlier generation of gods.

    _____

    _____

    _____

    _____

    _____

    _____

2. Retell the myth of the birth of Zeus. Be sure to include Cronus, Rhea, Amalthea, and the cornucopia.

    _____

    _____

    _____

3. Retell the myth of Jupiter and Europa.

   _____

   _____

   _____

4. Retell the myth of Mercury, Apollo, and the lyre.

   _____

   _____

   _____

5. What is the genitive of Jupiter? What is the ablative? Give an English expression that uses the ablative of Jupiter.

   _____

6. Find out information about the minor goddess Iris. Which goddess did Iris serve as messenger? What is Iris's symbol? At whose death did Iris assist according to Vergil in Book 4 of the *Aeneid*? What part of the human eye is the iris? What does the word "iridescent" mean? What colors are found in the blossom of an iris flower?

   _____

   _____

   _____

   _____

   _____

   _____

IV. Choose and circle the best answer from A, B, C, or D.

1. Quis sum? Ego sum dea potēns. Agrōs amō, et agricolās, frūmentum, frūctūsque cūrō.

A. Minerva	B. Ceres
C. Juno	D. Diana

2. A woman described as **Junoesque** is

A. stately	B. ugly
C. shy	D. articulate

3. Born under an olive tree on the island Delos, twin of the sun god, this goddess loved the mortal Endymion. She was in charge of the moon's path across the night sky and was the goddess of the hunt. What was this divinity's name?

   A. Diana   B. Minerva
   C. Vesta   D. Juno

4. The word **martial** comes from the name of the Roman god of

   A. the sea   B. the sun
   C. agriculture   D. war

5. This goddess of love and beauty was the mother of the hero Aeneas.

   A. Minerva   B. Vesta
   C. Diana   D. Venus

V. Just for fun.
Find a published image of each symbol. Describe or draw the symbol.

1. aegis

2. caduceus

3. trident

4. lyre

5.   Cerberus

6.   cornucopia

Greek Deities Review

Look at the chart below and see how many of the Greek divinities you know. Please note that words like "caduceus" are defined below the chart. To learn the names, realms, and symbols thoroughly, it is a good idea to make a flash card for each god or goddess.

	Greek Name	Realm	Symbols
1.	Zeus	king of gods and mortals	lightning bolt, eagle
2.	Hephaistos	blacksmith	hammer and anvil
3.	Hermes	messenger	winged hat and sandals, caduceus
4.	Poseidon	sea, earthquakes	dolphins, horses, trident
5.	Apollo	sun, music, archery, medicine	lyre, bow, sun chariot
6.	Ares	war	fierce dogs
7.	Hades	underworld, wealth	three-headed dog Cerberus, bident
8.	Hera	queen of gods, marriage	peacock
9.	Aphrodite	love, beauty	doves
10.	Demeter	agriculture	cornucopia
11.	Artemis	moon, hunting	bow, moon
12.	Athena	war, wisdom, weaving	owl, aegis
13.	Hestia	hearth, home	hearth fire

caduceus = winged staff

lyre = small stringed musical instrument resembling a harp

cornucopia = horn of plenty

trident = three-pronged spear

bident = two-pronged spear

aegis = shield with the image of the head of the Gorgon Medusa

*Greek Deity Match

Test yourself by matching the gods and goddesses with their attributes.

1. _____ Athena   A. king of gods and mortals

2. _____ Artemis   B. war

3. _____ Hermes   C. messenger, patron of thieves and merchants

4. _____ Aphrodite   D. war, wisdom, weaving

5. _____ Hera   E. sea, horses, earthquakes

6. _____ Hestia   F. hearth

7. _____ Ares   G. moon, hunting

8. _____ Zeus   H. love, beauty

9. _____ Apollo   I. sun, music, medicine

10. _____ Poseidon   J. queen of gods and mortals

Roman Deities Review

Now, here are the Roman names for the gods and goddesses; you already know their realms and symbols. To learn these names, it is a good idea to make another set of flash cards, one for each god or goddess.

Jupiter = Zeus
Vulcan = Hephaistos
Mercury = Hermes
Mars = Ares
Neptune = Poseidon
Apollo = Apollo
Juno = Hera
Vesta = Hestia
Venus = Aphrodite
Ceres = Demeter
Diana = Artemis
Minerva = Athena
Hades = Pluto

*Roman Deity Match

Test yourself by matching the Latin names of the gods and goddesses with their attributes.

1.	_____	Jupiter	A.	queen of gods and men, patron of weddings
2.	_____	Vulcan	B.	the hearth
3.	_____	Mercury	C.	love and beauty
4.	_____	Mars	D.	war, wisdom, and weaving
5.	_____	Neptune	E.	hunting and the moon
6.	_____	Apollo	F.	agriculture
7.	_____	Juno	G.	king of gods and men
8.	_____	Vesta	H.	music, medicine, and the sun
9.	_____	Venus	I.	patron of blacksmiths and craftsmen
10.	_____	Ceres	J.	messenger, patron of merchants and thieves
11.	_____	Diana	K.	the sea
12.	_____	Minerva	L.	war

CHAPTER 11
SCHOOL AND BOOK DERIVATIVES

Basic literacy was widespread in the Roman world. We can still see numerous graffiti on the walls of Pompeii. We also know that there were several public libraries in the city of Rome and that many educated men had private libraries of their own. The Villa of the Papyri in Herculaneum, for example, had an extensive library.

Roman youngsters, both boys and girls whose parents could afford it, learned their letters and simple arithmetic at home or in a little school. Apparently many Roman school teachers were noted for their strictness. Corporal punishment was commonplace. The poet Horace refers to his teacher as *plāgōsus* (fond of flogging). There is even a Latin verb *vāpulāre*, which means "take a beating." A wall painting from a house on the Via dell'Abbondanza in Pompeii shows a student being beaten. In the light of the sternness of Roman discipline, it seems surprising that the same Latin word *lūdus* means both "school" and "game." In English we find derivatives of *lūdus* in words like "interlude," "prelude," and "postlude." "Discipline" and "disciple," incidentally, are both derived from the Latin verb *discō* (learn).

More advanced education was normally reserved for wealthy Roman boys. A wealthy Roman boy often had a slave called a *paedagōgus* who accompanied him to school, sat in class with him, and helped him with his homework. In modern English, the word "pedagogy" refers to "the whole field of education." The word "education" is itself derived from the Latin verb *ēducō* meaning "to bring up, nurture, rear, lead out." In fact, Roman parents sometimes invoked a spirit called Educa, one of several minor deities who watched over the development of babies. Educa's name is obviously related to *ēducō*, and she was in charge of overseeing an infant's transition from milk to a diet of solid food.

A Roman teacher could illustrate math problems on an *abacus*, a small counting frame. A teacher might also make use of a table covered with sand. Geometric figures could be drawn with a stick in the sand, and small stones or pebbles could be used to illustrate math problems. The "small stones" used as counters were called *calculī*. The Latin word for "pebble" has given us the English word "calculus" (a branch of higher mathematics).

The Latin word for "sand" is *harēna*, which has come into English as the word "arena." Of course, today we think of an arena as an area surrounded by seating for spectators who have come to watch an athletic event or a show. A modern arena does not have sand on the floor, but in ancient Rome, sand was necessary in amphitheaters like the Colosseum to soak up and mask the blood that resulted from the gladiatorial spectacles.

Roman children learned to write with a *stilus* (a pointed stick) on a *tabella* (wax tablet). It is interesting that today we write on our electronic tablets with a stylus. *Tabellae* were used for all kinds of written records. Several small writing tablets could be fastened together as we sometimes fasten loose-leaf paper in a report. These were called *cōdicillī*, and the English word "codicil" means "an addition to a will." Literally a codicil is a "little *cōdex*." A *cōdex* was a book made of wooden blocks fastened together, so a *cōdicillus* is a scrap of writing on a small piece of writing material, used to add to or change something about a larger piece of writing.

A *scrība* (a skilled secretary) wrote not on a wax tablet, but rather on *charta* (paper). The English word "chart" is obviously derived from *charta*, while the English word "paper" is a derivative of *papȳrus*, "the reed from which paper was made." Each sheet of paper was laboriously made by weaving strips of papyrus together. The edges of the papyrus were then smoothed with a pumice stone. The sheets of papyrus were joined to make a *liber* (book or scroll) that contained the equivalent of between ten and twenty pages of a modern book. Another Latin word for "scroll or book" is *volūmen*, and you can see that *volūmen* is related to the verb *volvō* (to roll). A work like the *Aeneid* required twelve scrolls. Each scroll was labeled with a "tag" called a *titulus*. The scroll was rolled around a "stick" called an *umbilīcus*, and tied with ribbons. It might have a *membrāna* (cover). We can imagine the shelves of an ancient library filled with *capsae* (book boxes). A large number of scrolls was stored in each *capsa*.

A *scrība* wrote with a *penna* (pen). He would use ink made from soot and resin or from the liquid of a cuttle-fish. A mistake on a *tabella* could easily be corrected by smoothing it over with the blunt end of the *stilus*, but a mistake in ink had to be scraped off with a sharp knife. *Charta* was so expensive that sometimes whole scrolls were scraped clean and reused. Such a scroll is called a *palimpsestum* (palimpsest).

EXERCISES

I. Fill in the blank with the meaning of each English word. Some of the English meanings were discussed above, some may require a dictionary, and some you may know already or can guess.

Latin word	English word	Meaning of English
1. *liber, librī* (m.) = book	library	_____
2. *lūdus, -ī* (m.) = school, game	postlude	_____
3. *discō, -ere, didicī* = learn	discipline	_____
4. *paedagōgus, -ī* (m.) = tutor, guide	pedagogical	_____
5. *ēducō, -āre* = bring up, rear, nurture	education	_____
6. *arēna (harēna), -ae* (f.) = sand	arena	_____
7. *calculus, -ī* (m.) = pebble	calculus	_____
8. *stilus, -ī* (m.) = pen (for a wax tablet)	stylus	_____
9. *tabella, -ae* (f.) = wax tablet	tablet	_____
10. *cōdicillī, -ōrum* (m. pl.) = set of tablets	codicil	_____

11. *scrība, -ae* (m.) = scribe, secretary   scribe   _____

12. *charta, -ae* (f.) = paper   chart   _____

13. *papȳrus, -ī* (f.) = reed   papyrology   _____

14. *volūmen, volūminis* (n.) = scroll   voluminous   _____

15. *capsa, -ae* (f.) = book box   capsule   _____

16. *umbilīcus, -ī* (m.) = rod of a scroll   umbilical   _____

17. *titulus, -ī* (m.) = label   title   _____

18. *membrāna, -ae* (f.) = cover   membrane   _____

19. *penna, -ae* (f.) = pen, feather   penmanship   _____

20. *palimpsestum, -ī* (n.) = reused paper   palimpsest   _____

II. Choose and circle the best answer from A, B, C, or D.

1. What would a Roman keep in a *capsa*?

   A. food   B. wine
   C. scrolls   D. clothes

2. The English words **disciple** and **discipline** are derived from the Latin word *discō* that means to

   A. teach   B. learn
   C. dance   D. punish

3. You might find the phrase *ex libris* on a

   A. book plate   B. trophy
   C. plaque   D. gravestone

4. *Penna* and *stilus* are Latin words that refer to

   A. scribes   B. scrolls
   C. pens   D. tablets

5. **Calculus** means a branch of mathematics today; what does *calculus* mean in Latin?

   A. a pebble   B. sand
   C. an abacus   D. school

III. Answer briefly. NB: You may need to use a dictionary or an Internet site.

1. Explain the derivation of the English word "manuscript."

    _____

2. Give the meaning and principal parts of the Latin verb *currō*. Define the English derivative "cursive."
    Explain why Cicero's secretary Tiro called his shorthand "cursive."

    _____

    _____

3. What was the job of a Roman *capsārius*?

    _____

4. What is a *cōdex*? How is a *cōdex* different from a *volūmen*?

    _____

5. In Latin the word *cūnābula* means a cradle for a baby. To a rare book enthusiast what are "incunabula"?

    _____

6. Translate the phrase Magna Carta. What was the Magna Carta? Which English king was forced to
    sign the Magna Carta? In what year was the Magna Carta signed? Why is it an important document
    for Americans?

    _____

    _____

IV. Match the Latin word with its English meaning.

1. _____ *liber*   A. pen, feather
2. _____ *capsa*   B. learn
3. _____ *penna*   C. tutor
4. _____ *scrība*   D. rod of a scroll
5. _____ *discō*   E. roll
6. _____ *paedagōgus*   F. school, game
7. _____ *umbilīcus*   G. recycled paper
8. _____ *volvō*   H. secretary
9. _____ *lūdus*   I. book box
10. _____ *palimpsestum*   J. book

V. Translate these Latin phrases.

1. lapsus pennae   _____

2. docendo discitur   _____

3. ex libris   _____

VI. Just for fun.
Design a book plate with the words *Ex Libris* and your name, plus a design that reflects your personality or your taste in books.

CHAPTER 12
GEOGRAPHICAL DERIVATIVES

The word "geography" is Greek in origin: *geo–* comes from the Greek word for "earth," and *graphy* is derived from the Greek verb that means "to write." Latin geographical terms, however, have given us the roots of a number of interesting English words. For instance, the Latin for "world" is *orbis terrārum* (circle of lands), and in English an "orb" is "a sphere." As a Latin student, you can easily see that *terrārum* is the genitive plural of *terra* (land). The word "Mediterranean" is a combination of *medius* (middle) plus *terra*, and the Mediterranean is, in fact, at the center of the lands controlled by Rome. Of course, you probably know that the Romans themselves referred to the Mediterranean as *Mare Nostrum* (our sea).

Pelagus is another Latin word for "sea." It gives us the English word "pelagic" (living in or pertaining to the open sea). An "estuary," by contrast, refers to "an arm of the sea at the mouth of a river." The word "estuary" is derived from *aestus* (heat, boiling, tide), and unlike an inland waterway, an "estuary" is subject to tides.

Some Latin place-names are exactly the same in English but indicate areas with very different boundaries. To us, "Africa" means a whole continent, but to a Roman, *Āfrica* meant the territory along the coast of North Africa. Similarly, *Asia* in Latin refers only to the area that today we call "Asia Minor." It is interesting that the English word "continent" (a large land mass) is derived from the Latin phrase *terra continēns* meaning "land holding together."

Two large islands in the Mediterranean just west of Italy, Corsica and Sardinia, are still called by their Latin names. The Latin word *īnsula* (island) gives us the derivative "insular," which means "narrow-minded." A synonym of "insular" in English is the word "provincial," which comes from the Latin word *prōvincia* (an area outside Rome governed by a Roman official).

In the opening paragraph of Book 1 of *Dē Bellō Gallicō* Caesar sets the scene for his first campaign as governor of Gaul (modern France). He describes in detail the topography of the area where he will conduct the operation. Obviously, geography was important to a general planning strategy, but it also seems clear that Caesar's audience at home in Rome was interested in learning about a part of the world largely unfamiliar to them.

When a Roman author like Caesar is orienting his readers, he often uses the names of winds for the points of the compass. Thus, *Boreās*, the name of the wind that blows from the north, means "north," while *Auster*, the wind that blows from the south, can simply mean "south," and *Zephyrus* (the west wind) means "west." Besides the names of winds, the Romans also expressed directions in terms of the sun or stars. The Latin word *merīdiēs*, which can mean "noon or midday," also means "south," since the sun is visible to the south at noon. In the same way, *occidēns* (setting) and *sōlis occāsus* (sunset) indicate a westerly direction, and *oriēns* (rising) means "east." The English words "occidental" (western) and "oriental" (eastern) are derived from these Latin words. Caesar also uses *septentriō* or *septentriōnēs* for "north" because *Septentriōnēs* was the Latin name for the seven-star constellation we call the "Big Dipper," and the North Star can be located by following an imaginary line from the far edge of the bowl of the dipper.

The Latin word for "map" is *charta*, and you can see that the English word "cartographer" (mapmaker) is derived from *charta*. Another Latin word sometimes used for a "map" is *mappa*. Thus, *mappa mundī* is "a map of the world." And you may have learned that *mappa* can also mean "a napkin."

EXERCISES

I. Fill in the blank with the meaning of each English word. Some of the English meanings were discussed above, some may require a dictionary, and some you may know already or can guess.

Latin word	English word	Meaning of English
1. *orbis terrārum* = world	orb	_____
2. *oriēns, -ntis* = east	orient	_____
3. *occidēns, -ntis* = west	occidental	_____
4. *Zephyrus, -ī* (m.) = West Wind, west	zephyr	_____
5. *Boreās, -ae* (m.) = North Wind, north	aurora borealis	_____
6. *merīdiēs, -diēī* (m.) = noon, south	meridian	_____
7. *Auster, -strī* (m.) = South Wind, south	Australia	_____
8. *mare, maris* (n.) = sea	marine	_____
9. *pelagus, -ī* (n.) = sea	pelagic	_____
10. *īnsula, -ae* (f.) = island	insulate	_____
11. *aestus, -ūs* (m.) = heat, tide	estuary	_____
12. *flūmen, -inis* (n.) = river	flume	_____
13. *rīvus, -ī* (m.) = river	derivative	_____
14. *charta, -ae* (f.) = paper, map	cartography	_____
15. *mīlle passūs* = mile	mile	_____
16. *via, -ae* (f.) = road	trivia	_____
17. *prōvincia, -ae* (f.) = province	provincial	_____
18. *terra, -ae* (f.) = land	terrain	_____
	extraterrestrial	_____

19. *patria, -ae* (f.) = fatherland   repatriate   _____

      expatriate   _____

      patriotic   _____

20. *mappa, -ae* (f.) = map, napkin   map   _____

21. *mundus, -ī* (m.) = world   mundane   _____

22. *contineō, -ēre, -uī, contentum* = keep in, hold together   transcontinental   _____

II. Use a dictionary if needed to find the meaning of these phrases.

1. ante meridiem (A.M.)   _____

2. post meridiem (P.M.)   _____

3. sic transit gloria mundi   _____

III. Use a Latin dictionary if needed to find the English translation of the names of these rivers.

1. *Dānuvius*   _____

2. *Rhēnus*   _____

3. *Rubicō*   _____

4. *Tiberis*   _____

IV. Use a Latin dictionary if needed to find the English translation of the names of these mountains.

1. *Alpēs*   _____

2. *Appennīnus*   _____

3. *Pȳrēnaeī*   _____

V. Use a Latin dictionary if needed to find the English translation of the names of these areas.

1. *Britannia*   _____

2. *Calēdonia*   _____

3. *Eurōpa*   _____

4. *Gallia*   _____

5. *Graecia*   _____

6. *Hibernia*   _____

7. *Hispānia*   _____

8. *Ībēria*   _____

9. *Lūsitānia*   _____

10. *Aegyptus*   _____

11. *Parthia*   _____

12. *Syria*   _____

VI. Choose and circle the best answer from A, B, C, or D.

1. *Zephyrus, Boreās,* and *Auster* are names of

   A. rivers   B. towns
   C. mountains   D. winds

2. The Latin phrase *sōlis occāsūs* means

   A. north   B. south
   C. east   D. west

3. A person described as **provincial** is

   A. optimistic   B. insular
   C. rich   D. curious

4. The Iberian peninsula includes

   A. England and Scotland   B. Spain and Portugal
   C. Belgium and France   D. Albania and Greece

5. Which animal might be described as **pelagic**?

   A. a fish   B. a cow
   C. a goat   D. a bird

VII. Answer briefly. NB: You may need to use a dictionary or an Internet site.

1. What is the prime meridian?

_____

2. Give the Latin roots of the English words "latitude" and "longitude."

    _____

3. Translate *mīlle passūs* literally. What is the plural of *mīlle passūs* in Latin? How far is a Roman mile compared to an American mile?

    _____

    _____

4. Find information about the Titan named Atlas. Write a brief summary of what you have found. Be sure to retell the story of Atlas's encounter with Hercules. Include the location of the mountain range that bears Atlas's name and the meaning of the English word "atlas."

    _____

    _____

    _____

    _____

5. Retell the myth of the nymph Europa, who gave her name to the continent of Europe.

    _____

    _____

    _____

6. The Rubicon River in northeastern Italy marked an important political boundary during the Roman Republic. Find information about Julius Caesar's decision to cross the Rubicon in 49 BCE. What Latin phrase is associated with this event?

    _____

    _____

    _____

7. In English "ocean" means "a vast body of salt water." Find the meaning of the Latin word *ōceanus*. Explain briefly how the two words are different in concept. Now, look up the marine god Oceanus in a mythology handbook. Explain why it is appropriate that Oceanus gave his name to a mythical body of water surrounding all the lands of the earth.

    _____

    _____

    _____

8.   In Latin *paene* means "almost," and *īnsula* means "island." In English a "peninsula" is "an area of land surrounded on three sides by water." Look at a map of the Roman Empire, and find three peninsulas. Write out the names of the three peninsulas in Latin.

9.   Sometimes in English the ocean is called "the deep." Give the Latin adjective that means "high" or "deep." Then translate the English phrase "on the deep" into Latin.

VIII. Just for fun.

1.   Find an image of the scepter and orb carried by English monarchs as symbols of their power. Share the picture with your classmates.

2.   Find a map of the roads of the Roman Empire. Enlarge and copy it. Label the roads, cities, towns, islands, mountains, rivers, and seas in Latin.

CHAPTER 13
HALLOWEEN DERIVATIVES

Trick-or-treating, funny costumes, and bags of candy make Halloween a lot of fun. Halloween is also a perfect time to tell scary ghost stories. A famous ghost story that you might want to read or translate at Halloween is one written in the first century CE by the Roman author Pliny the Younger. You may already be familiar with Pliny's letters describing the eruption of Mount Vesuvius in 79 CE, or you may have read his letter to the emperor Trajan about the imperial policy toward Christians. The ghost story also comes from one of Pliny's letters. In writing to an old friend, Pliny describes an elegant and spacious house in Athens that is being offered for sale or rent at a suspiciously low price. Pliny has discovered that the price is low because the house is haunted! He describes the *larva* (ghost) as an old man who is in the habit of clanging *vincula* (chains) at night. The skeleton of the ghost is eventually found in a shallow grave, exhumed, and properly buried so the ghost can be at rest and cease to haunt the house.

It is interesting that the Latin word *larva* has come into English meaning "the wingless stage in an insect's development before it has undergone metamorphosis." The wingless immature insect is a ghost or specter of the fully formed adult that it will eventually become. Another word for "ghost or shade" in Latin is *umbra*. One English derivative from *umbra* is the word "adumbrate," but it does not have anything to do with ghosts; it means "to foreshadow or foretell an event." Similarly, "umbrage" does not refer to a ghost but instead means "resentment" because someone who takes umbrage may look as though a shadow has passed over his or her face. Another English derivative from *umbra* is "penumbra" meaning "partial shade." The prefix *pen–* comes, as Latin students know, from the Latin word *paene* meaning "almost."

The word Pliny uses for the ghost's chains is *vincula*. You may know "vinculum," the singular of *vincula*, from math class. A "vinculum" means "a stroke drawn over several terms to show that they should be taken together," i.e., they are chained together.

Pliny explains that the *ossa* (bones) of the ghost have to be dug up out of the earth in order for them to be reburied. The English word that means "to dig up out of the earth" is "exhume." *Ex* is the Latin preposition meaning "out of, from," and *humus* means "earth." When you read that someone has gained posthumous fame, you know that this time the prefix is the Latin preposition *post* meaning "after," so "posthumous" means "after death and burial."

Pliny does not mention that his ghost's burial place was marked with a *lapis* (a gravestone, a stone), but there are several interesting English derivatives from *lapis*. For example, a building that is "in bad repair" might be described as "dilapidated," as though stones were falling down from its walls. A jeweler who works with precious stones can be called a "lapidary," and a succinct and elegant style of writing may be described as "lapidary." The work of a "lapidary," who shapes and polishes jewels, can be compared to the work of an author whose "lapidary" style also requires careful cutting and polishing.

The ghost in Pliny's letter did not wear a mask as many trick-or-treaters do on Halloween. Instead, in the ancient world it was actors who wore *persōnae* (masks). A list of the cast of characters in a play was known as the *dramatis persōnae*. Each actor played several roles in Roman dramas, and masks helped an actor portray different characters. In addition, only men were actors so a mask was helpful for an actor playing a female role. The word *persōna* may also reflect the fact that a mask could amplify the *sonus* (sound) as it was projected *per* (through) the mouthpiece of the mask. So next Halloween, as you put on your *persōna* to trick-or-treat, remember that, like an ancient actor, you are preparing to play a role.

EXERCISES

I. Fill in the blank with the meaning of each English word. Some of the English meanings were discussed above, some may require a dictionary, and some you may know already or can guess.

Latin word	English word	Meaning of English
1. *larva, -ae* (f.) = ghost	larva	_____
2. *umbra, -ae* (f.) = shade, shadow, ghost	umbrella	_____
	adumbrate	_____
	penumbra	_____
	umbrage	_____
3. *vinculum, -ī* (n.) = chain, fetters	vinculum	_____
4. *humus, -ī* (f.) = ground, earth	exhume	_____
	posthumous	_____
5. *sepulcrum, -ī* (n.) = tomb	sepulcher	_____
6. *os, ossis* (n.) = bone	ossify	_____
7. *fraus, fraudis* (f.) = trick, deceit	fraudulent	_____
8. *dēlectātiō, -ōnis* (f.) = treat	delectable	_____
9. *persōna, -ae* (f.) = mask	impersonate	_____
10. *lapis, lapidis* (m.) = stone, gravestone	dilapidated	_____
	lapidary	_____
11. *catēna, -ae* (f.) = chain	concatenation	_____

II.
Use a dictionary to find the meanings of these phrases.

1. requiescat in pace (R.I.P.) _____

2. dramatis personae _____

3. exeunt omnes _____

4. persona non grata _____

III.
Answer briefly. NB: You may need to use a dictionary or an Internet site.

1. Find the English meaning and the location of these bones: *tībia, ulna, patella.*

   _____

   _____

2. What phase in an insect's metamorphosis is called the "larval" stage? What does *larva* mean in Latin? Why is "larval" an appropriate description of this stage?

   _____

   _____

3. What phase in an insect's metamorphosis is called the "pupa" stage? What does *pūpa* mean in Latin? Why is "pupa" an appropriate description of this stage?

   _____

   _____

4. Translate the phrase "trick or treat" into Latin.

   _____

IV. Match the Latin word with its English meaning.

1. _____ *umbra*
2. _____ *persōna*
3. _____ *humus*
4. _____ *sepulcrum*
5. _____ *vinculum*
6. _____ *os, ossis*
7. _____ *lapis*
8. _____ *larva*
9. _____ *fraus*
10. _____ *dēlectātiō*

A. treat
B. trick
C. ghost
D. stone, gravestone
E. bone
F. chain
G. tomb
H. earth
I. mask
J. shade, shadow, ghost

V. Choose and circle the best answer from A, B, C, or D.

1. The English words **umbrage**, **penumbra**, and **adumbrate** are derived from the Latin word that means

    A. sun
    C. shade
    B. stars
    D. number

2. The English words **inhume**, **exhume**, and **posthumous** are derived from the Latin word that means

    A. earth
    C. mortal
    B. fame
    D. death

3. If someone describes a special dish as **delectable**, it means the dish was

    A. salty
    C. baked
    B. cold
    D. delicious

4. **Dilapidated** and **lapidary** are derivatives of the Latin word that means

    A. stone
    C. bone
    B. style
    D. mask

5. You would be most likely to find an example of a **vinculum** in a book about

    A. cooking
    C. astronomy
    B. math
    D. gardening

VI. Just for fun.

1. Read in translation a story by an ancient author of an encounter with a werewolf. The author is Petronius, the work is the *Satyricon*, section 62.

2. Translate the word "Halloween" into Latin. Research its derivation. Does the word "Halloween" have Latin roots?

3. Prepare a poster with an image of a skeleton. Label all the bones in Latin.

CHAPTER 14
THANKSGIVING DERIVATIVES

In the United States, the fourth Thursday in November is a special holiday set aside for giving thanks. And for many families the most important part of Thanksgiving is eating a big dinner together. In ancient Rome, by contrast, there was no national day of thanksgiving, and in fact, the Romans could never have eaten many of the foods we enjoy at Thanksgiving nowadays. Turkey, potatoes, sweet potatoes, corn, squash, tomatoes, or desserts sweetened with sugar or flavored with chocolate were unknown in the Roman world because they are products of the Americas.

Moreover, butter was not used in cooking, only in medicine as a healing salve, and since sugar was unknown, *mel* (honey) was used as a sweetener. Honey was added to dishes such as *ōva mellīta*, a concoction of beaten *ōva* (eggs) with pepper and honey on top. The English word "omelet" is derived from this delicacy.

Studies of the skeletons found in the ancient city of Herculaneum indicate that the people there were healthy and well nourished. There was little tooth decay because there were few *dulcia* (sweets), and chewy bread meant well-developed jaws and teeth. It is interesting that the English word "companion" comes from the Latin word *pānis* (bread) because someone with whom you break bread is your companion or friend.

While working people often ate at fast food counters, as the number of *thermopōlia* (bars) in Pompeii and Herculaneum attests, wealthy Romans preferred elaborate meals prepared at home in the *culīna* (kitchen). You can see that the English word "culinary" comes from *culīna*. The kitchen staff in a large household often included a slave in charge of chopping up the food that was to be served. Such a slave was known as a *scissor*.

We know quite a lot about some of the dishes that Roman cooks prepared because an ancient cookbook by a Roman writer named Apicius still exists. It is clear from Apicius's recipes that the Romans enjoyed a varied diet. They ate both *carō* (meat) and *piscēs* (fish) and a variety of *holera* (vegetables). They can be described as omnivores!

If a modern American family says that their Thanksgiving dinner was delicious "from soup to nuts," they mean that the meal was tasty from start to finish. Similarly, the Latin phrase *ab ovo usque ad mala* (from eggs to apples) is a description of an entire Roman meal: the appetizer might consist of hard-boiled eggs; apples or another fruit could be served as dessert.

EXERCISES

I. Fill in the blank with the meaning of each English word. Some of the English meanings were discussed on the previous page, some may require a dictionary, and some you may know already or can guess.

Latin word	English word	Meaning of English
1. *grātiae, -ārum* (f. pl.) = thanks	grace	
	gratitude	
	ingrate	
2. *carō, carnis* (f.) = meat, flesh	carnivore	
	incarnation	
3. *herba, -ae* (f.) = grass, vegetation	herbivore	
4. *mel, mellis* (n.) = honey	melody	
5. *oleum, -ī* (n.) = oil	petroleum	
6. *pānis, pānis* (m.) = bread	companion	
7. *dulcis, -e* = sweet	dulcimer	
8. *culīna, -ae* (f.) = kitchen	culinary	
9. *vīnum, -ī* (n.) = wine	wine	
10. *aqua, -ae* (f.) = water	aqueduct	
11. *crustula, -ae* (f.) = cookie	crust	
12. *scissor, -ōris* (m.) = skilled chopper	scissors	
13. *ōvum, -ī* (n.) = egg	oval	
14. *prandium, -ī* (n.) = lunch	postprandial	
15. *piscis, -is* (m.) = fish	piscatorial	

II. Translate these phrases. NB: you may need to use a dictionary or an Internet site.

1. cum grano salis _____

2. in vino veritas _____

3. de gustibus non est disputandum _____

4. ab ovo usque ad mala _____

5. cornucopia _____

III. Match the Latin word with its English meaning.

1. _____ *ōvum*   A. fish
2. _____ *mel*   B. lunch
3. _____ *carō*   C. meat
4. _____ *culīna*   D. egg
5. _____ *piscis*   E. honey
6. _____ *prandium*   F. water
7. _____ *vīnum*   G. cookie
8. _____ *aqua*   H. kitchen
9. _____ *crustula*   I. wine
10. _____ *oleum*   J. oil

IV. Answer briefly. NB: You may need to use a dictionary or an Internet site.

1. Why was it necessary for a wealthy Roman to employ a *scissor*, a slave skilled at chopping up food? Hint: What eating utensils were lacking in the ancient world?

_____

_____

2. If an "aqueduct" carries water, what is the function of a "viaduct"?

_____

3. What is the Latin word for "dining room"? How many couches did it usually contain?

_____

4. What does *agō grātiās* mean in Latin?

_____

5. What is a "cornucopia?" Why would it be an appropriate table decoration for a Thanksgiving dinner?

_____

_____

6. The English word "recipe" is an imperative of the Latin verb *recipiō*. What does *recipe* mean literally? How is the word *recipe* abbreviated in a modern pharmacy?

_____

7. Give the principal parts of the Latin verb *edō* (eat). Define the English words "edible" and "comestible."

   _____

   _____

8. An important element of many Roman dishes was a sauce called *garum*. Find out what the ingredients were of *garum* and how it was made.

   _____

   _____

9. The Latin word for "table" is *mensa*. If two animals or two plants are described by a biologist as being in a "commensal" relationship, what does that mean?

   _____

V. Choose and circle the best answer from A, B, C, or D.

1. In what room of a Roman house would the cook prepare dinner?

   A. *trīclīnium*   B. *ātrium*

   C. *iānua*   D. *culīna*

2. A **piscatorial** expert would most likely deliver a lecture about

   A. fish   B. birds

   C. trees   D. bees

3. When would someone take a **postprandial** stroll?

   A. before dinner   B. after lunch

   C. at night   D. at dawn

4. Where might a Roman child be heard asking, "Dā mihi crustulam, quaesō!"?

   A. in the garden   B. at the beach

   C. in the kitchen   D. in the Forum

5. A **cornucopia** decorating a dining room table ready for a Thanksgiving dinner is most likely filled with

   A. napkins   B. fruits and vegetables

   C. candles   D. salt and pepper

6. Which food was never served at a Roman meal?

   A. bread   B. eggs

   C. tomatoes   D. honey

7. The English words **omnivore**, **carnivore**, and **herbivore** are derived from the Latin verb *vorō* meaning

   A. cultivate   B. prefer
   C. devour   D. wish

8. The author of an ancient cookbook in Latin was

   A. Tacitus   B. Ovid
   C. Apicius   D. Lucretius

9. The Latin phrase *ab ovo usque ad mala* means

   A. from start to finish   B. there is no accounting for tastes
   C. to the stars through difficulties   D. out of many one

VI. Just for fun.

Look at the menu below. The dishes suggested here were taken from Apicius's famous cookbook. Find a translation of Apicius's work and make up a menu for an elegant Roman dinner like this one. Be sure to include three courses. Does a call for pizza (*ofellae*) suddenly seem appealing?

Appetizers
Jellyfish and eggs
Sow's udders stuffed with salted sea urchins
Patina of brains cooked with milk and eggs
Boiled tree fungi with peppered fish-fat sauce
Sea urchins with spices, honey, oil, and egg sauce

Main Course
Fallow deer roasted with onion sauce, rue, Jericho dates, raisins, oil, and honey
Boiled ostrich with sweet sauce
Turtle dove boiled in its feathers
Roast parrot
Dormice stuffed with pork and pine kernels
Ham boiled with figs and bay leaves, rubbed with honey, baked in pastry crust
Flamingo boiled with dates

Dessert
Fricassee of roses with pastry
Stoned dates stuffed with nuts and pine kernels, fried in honey
Hot African sweet-wine cakes with honey

Hadas, Moses, *Imperial Rome.*
(New York, Time Life Books, 1971, p. 85)

PART III

Grammar-Related Derivatives

CHAPTER 15

FIRST AND SECOND DECLENSION MASCULINE AND FEMININE NOUN DERIVATIVES

Many English derivatives from first and second declension masculine and feminine Latin words are almost the same in both languages: the Latin word *poēta* is "poet" in English, and the Latin word *epistula* is "epistle" (letter) in English. Often a Latin word like *via* comes directly into English. Of course, *via* in Latin means "a road" like the Via Appia while "via" in English has an additional meaning or connotation: it is used as a preposition meaning "through" or "by."

The English word "sylvan" (pertaining to woods or a forest) is not spelled exactly like its Latin root *silva*, but the two words sound similar so it is easy to see the connection between them. It is interesting to see that spelling appearing in place-names like Transylvania and Pennsylvania. There is even a county in Virginia named after the colonial governor Alexander Spotswood. The county is called Spotsylvania.

Sometimes, the prefix of an English word can clarify the meaning of an English derivative. For instance, the Latin word *patria* means "homeland" and the prefix *ex* means "out of," so "expatriates" are "people who are not living in their homeland." You probably know that American authors like Ernest Hemingway and F. Scott Fitzgerald, who lived in France in the 1920s, are called "expatriates" or "expats." Similarly, an alien living in a foreign country without a visa might be "repatriated" (deported and sent back to one's country of origin).

A single English derivative can often help you remember a pair of Latin words. For example, "amicable" meaning "friendly" is a derivative of both *amīca* and *amīcus* because both are words for "friend," one female, the other male. Similarly, *dea* and *deus* are both "deities," one a goddess, one a god, so "deification" (elevation to the rank of god) is a good way to remember both words.

It can be useful to expand your English vocabulary by finding more derivatives of the Latin words in this lesson. "Aquarium" is certainly an obvious derivative of *aqua*, but why not also learn the English words "aqueduct," "aquifer," "aquamarine," "aquatic," "aquaculture," and "aqua vitae?" *Terra* is the root of "terrarium," but why not pick up "terrestrial," "extraterrestrial," "terra cotta," "terrain," and "terrace"? One Latin word can open the way to a rich and varied English vocabulary!

EXERCISES

I.

Fill in the blank with the meaning of each English word. Some of the English meanings were discussed above, some may require a dictionary, and some you may know already or can guess.

Latin word	English word	Meaning of English
1. *amīca, -ae* (f.) = friend	amicable	_____
2. *epistula, -ae* (f.) = letter	epistle	_____
3. *ancilla, -ae* (f.) = slave woman	ancillary	_____
4. *aqua, -ae* (f.) = water	aquarium	_____
5. *fēmina, -ae* (f.) = woman	feminine	_____
6. *patria, -ae* (f.) = fatherland	patriot	_____
	expatriate	_____
7. *fāma, -ae* (f.) = rumor, reputation	defamation	_____
8. *dea, -ae* (f.) = goddess	deify	_____
9. *silva, -ae* (f.) = woods, forest	sylvan	_____
10. *terra, -ae* (f.) = land, earth	terrarium	_____
11. *unda, -ae* (f.) = wave	undulation	_____
	abundant	_____
12. *via, -ae* (f.) = way, road	viaduct	_____
	deviate	_____
13. *vīta, -ae* (f.) = life	vital	_____
14. *īnsula, -ae* (f.) = island	insular	_____
15. *poēta, -ae* (m.) = poet	poetic	_____
16. *agricola, -ae* (m.) = farmer	agriculture	_____
17. *nauta, -ae* (m.) = sailor	nautical	_____
18. *amīcus, -ī* (m.) = friend	amiable	_____
19. *lēgātus, -ī* (m.) = lieutenant	legate	_____
20. *nūntius, -ī* (m.) = messenger, news	enunciate	_____

21. *vir, -ī* (m.) = man, husband   virile   _____

22. *deus, deī* (m.) = god   deification   _____

23. *puer, -ī* (m.) = boy   puerile   _____

II. Translate these phrases. NB: You may need to use a dictionary or an Internet site.

1. terra incognita   _____

2. terra firma   _____

3. amicus curiae   _____

4. ars longa, vita brevis   _____

III. Match the Latin word with its English meaning.

1. _____	*ancilla*	A.	fatherland, homeland
2. _____	*patria*	B.	man
3. _____	*dea*	C.	life
4. _____	*silva*	D.	earth
5. _____	*vīta*	E.	road
6. _____	*nūntius*	F.	boy
7. _____	*terra*	G.	goddess
8. _____	*puer*	H.	woods, forest
9. _____	*via*	I.	messenger, news
10. _____	*vir*	J.	slave woman

IV.

Answer briefly. NB: you may need to use a dictionary or an Internet site.

1. Most of the first declension nouns are feminine, but there are a few exceptions that are masculine. It is easy to remember this small group of exceptions if you think that these masculine first declension nouns are a PAIN. Each letter of "pain" stands for a masculine first declension noun: *poēta*, *agricola*, *incola*, and *nauta*. Give the meaning of each word.

   poēta _____

   agricola _____

   incola _____

   nauta _____

   NB: You may know that the Latin words *pīrāta*, *scrība*, and *āthlēta* also belong in this group.

2. Name the Quaker leader whose name plus the Latin word for "woods, forest" appears in the name of an important mid-Atlantic state.

   _____

3. What is an *amīcus cūriae* brief? Why would someone file an *amīcus* brief with a court?

   _____

   _____

4. *Īnsula* means "island" in Latin, and *paene* means "almost." What is an "almost island" in English?

   _____

5. *Trivium* in Latin means "a crossroad." Why does "trivia" in English mean "unimportant trifles?"

   _____

6. "Redundant" means "superfluous, unnecessary repetition in expressing a thought." What Latin word meaning "wave" is at the root of "redundant"?

   _____

V.

Choose and circle the best answer from A, B, C, or D.

1. The words **patriot**, **expatriate**, and **repatriate** are derived from the Latin word that means

   A. petition   B. part

   C. homeland   D. habitat

2. What did you receive if your grandmother sent you an **epistle**?

   A. a book   B. a pen
   C. a bookmark   D. a letter

3. Which animal would be most at home in a **sylvan** environment?

   A. a sheep   B. a fox
   C. a fish   D. a cow

4. The work of the vice president of a company is **ancillary** to that of the president and board.

   A. auxiliary   B. challenging
   C. vital   D. comparable

5. If your older sister describes your behavior as **puerile**, she means that it is

   A. entertaining   B. childish
   C. aggressive   D. demanding

6. **Enunciation**, **annunciation**, and **pronunciation** are all related to the Latin word that means

   A. orator   B. politician
   C. vendor   D. messenger

CHAPTER 16
SECOND DECLENSION NEUTER NOUN DERIVATIVES

The idea of having a gender assigned to places and things often seems puzzling to English speakers. After all, in English only nouns for people (and ships) are masculine or feminine, and none are neuter. Furthermore, it seems odd that in Latin tables or tablets or doors are feminine while books are masculine. It can be helpful, therefore, to think of gender in a Latin grammar context as a category like red, white, or blue. Sometimes the category will seem to align logically with a word: e.g., *fēmina* (woman) and *puella* (girl) are feminine, while *puer* (boy) and *vir* (man) are masculine, and many second declension neuter nouns, like *dōnum* (gift) are indeed things.

Second declension neuter nouns are easy to identify because the nominative and accusative singular almost always end in –*um*, and both the nominative and accusative plural end in the letter –*a*. You might find it helpful to remember these endings if you know that the word "datum" in English means "a single bit of information" while "data," the plural of "datum," means "a whole collection of facts." Similarly, the word "media," meaning "a method of communication like television," is simply the plural of "medium."

Sometimes, it is easy to see a connection between a Latin word like *praemium* and its English derivative if you remember that a diphthong like –*ae* often becomes an –*e* in English. Thus, "premium" is really the same word as *praemium*. You can see this process at work with *aedificium* (building) and "edifice," the English word for "a big building." Of course, "edification" in English does not literally refer to constructing a building; it means "building up morally."

One particularly interesting neuter noun in Latin is *verbum*. You might logically assume that *verbum* in Latin means "an action or state of being" as "verb" does in English. *Verbum*, however, has the broader, more general meaning of "word," and English derivatives like "verbose" (wordy) and "verbal" (articulate) reflect this.

An important neuter noun that is easy to connect with other Latin words is *rēgnum* (kingdom). You probably know that *rēgina, -ae* (f.) means "queen," and *rēx, rēgis* (m.) means "king." There is even an adjective *rēgius* meaning "royal." And you may well know the verb *regō*, "rule."

You also probably know the Latin for some of the rooms of a Roman house like *culīna* for "kitchen." Many such as *trīclīnium* (dining room), *ātrium* (formal parlor), *peristȳlium* (courtyard), *vestibulum* (hallway, entryway) are neuter. The father's study where he kept his *tabellae* (tablets) is the *tablīnum*, and a bedroom that was very small like a cubicle is a *cubiculum*.

Frūmentum (grain) is another interesting neuter noun. *Frūmentum* is often mentioned in Caesar's *Dē Bellō Gallicō,* his account of his campaigns in Gaul, because the Roman army needed a constant supply of grain. The word *frūmentum* can mean wheat, spelt, oats, or barley. It does not include corn because maize is a New World product unknown to the Romans. The English word "frumenty" means "a kind of hot cereal made from wheat" eaten by early settlers in New England.

EXERCISES

I. Fill in the blank with the meaning of each English word. Some of the English meanings were discussed above, some may require a dictionary, and some you may know already or can guess.

	Latin noun	*English word*	*Meaning of English*
1.	*aedificium, -ī* (n.) = building	edifice	_____
		edification	_____
2.	*auxilium, -ī* (n.) = help, aid	auxiliary	_____
3.	*bellum, -ī* (n.) = war	bellicose	_____
		belligerent	_____
4.	*caelum, -ī* (n.) = sky, heaven	celestial	_____
5.	*cōnsilium, -ī* (n.) = plan, advice	counsel	_____
6.	*cubiculum, -ī* (n.) = bedroom	cubicle	_____
7.	*dōnum, -ī* (n.) = gift	donate	_____
8.	*frūmentum, -ī* (n.) = grain	frumenty	_____
9.	*perīculum, -ī* (n.) = danger	peril	_____
10.	*praemium, -ī* (n.) = reward	premium	_____
11.	*rēgnum, -ī* (n.) = kingdom	regal	_____
12.	*sepulcrum, -ī* (n.) = tomb	sepulcher	_____
13.	*signum, -ī* (n.) = signal, banner, standard	signal	_____
14.	*tablīnum, -ī* (n.) = study	tablet	_____
15.	*verbum, -ī* (n.) = word	verbose	_____
16.	*vīnum, -ī* (n.) = wine	viniferous	_____
17.	*odium, -ī* (n.) = hate	odious	_____
18.	*ōtium, -ī* (n.) = leisure	otiose	_____

II. Translate these phrases. NB: you may need to use a dictionary or an Internet site.

1. in hoc signo vinces   _____

2. verbum sapientibus satis est   _____

3. in vino veritas   _____

III. Match the Latin word with its English meaning.

1. _____ *signum*   A. word
2. _____ *cōnsilium*   B. study
3. _____ *vīnum*   C. help, aid
4. _____ *perīculum*   D. signal
5. _____ *auxilium*   E. plan
6. _____ *verbum*   F. wine
7. _____ *sepulcrum*   G. danger
8. _____ *dōnum*   H. gift
9. _____ *cubiculum*   I. tomb
10. _____ *tablīnum*   J. bedroom

IV. Answer briefly. NB: you may need to use a dictionary or an Internet site.

1. Define each of these English words.

   council   _____

   counsel   _____

   consul   _____

   Which of the three English words can be a definition of the Latin word *cōnsilium*?

   _____

2. "Celestial" in English means "heavenly." What second declension neuter noun means "sky, heaven"?

   _____

3. *Signum* means "signal, standard, banner." What is a *signifer*?

   _____

4. One of the officials in Rome was an aedile (*aedīlis*). What were an aedile's duties?

    _____

    _____

5. The phrase *ante bellum* literally means "before the war" in English. To an American, which war does the phrase refer to?

    _____

6. What is the meaning of the Latin word *vulgus*? What is its genitive? To what declension does *vulgus* belong? What gender is *vulgus*?

    _____

    _____

V. Choose and circle the best answer from A, B, C, or D.

1. Based on your knowledge of the meaning of the Latin word *auxilium*, what does **auxiliary** mean in English?

    A. dangerous   B. helpful

    C. regal   D. exploratory

2. A *tablīnum*, a *cubiculum*, and a *triclīnium* would most likely be found in a Roman

    A. temple   B. shop

    C. garden   D. house

3. *Aedīlis*, *aedificō*, and *aedificium* come from the Latin word that means to

    A. sponsor   B. play

    C. read   D. build

4. **Frumenty** is a dish made of

    A. fruit   B. fish

    C. grain   D. cabbage

5. *Rēx*, *rēgīna*, and *rēgnum* are Latin words from the Latin verb that means

    A. rebel   B. arise

    C. return   D. rule

VI. Just for fun.

Find a floorplan for a typical Roman house in your textbook, in a book on Roman life, or on the Internet. Copy the plan and label each room in Latin. Include a legend with the translation of the Latin names for the rooms. Then, make a floorplan of your own house or apartment. Label the rooms in English.

CHAPTER 17
THIRD DECLENSION MASCULINE AND FEMININE NOUN DERIVATIVES

The third declension is the largest of the five declensions of Latin nouns. A substantial number of third declension nouns are cognates whose meanings are easy to remember because they closely resemble their English counterparts. The third declension also includes a variety of abstract nouns that have provided the roots for some interesting concepts in English.

All three genders are represented in the third declension. In addition, you will note that *cīvis*, the Latin word for "citizen," is designated as common gender (c.) because both men and women in Rome were citizens. Women could not vote in the citizen assemblies or hold official positions, but could, nonetheless, be citizens. A *cīvis*, therefore, could be either a man or a woman.

Most nouns ending in –*or* are masculine. These masculine third declension nouns include *timor* (fear), which obviously gives us the English word "timorous" (fearful) and *labor* (work), which gives us "laborious" (painstaking, difficult) or "elaborate" (intricate, highly crafted). A few third declension words that end in –*or*, e.g., *uxor* (wife) and *soror* (sister), are feminine because they refer to females. The English word "uxorious" means "doting on one's wife," while "sorority," a derivative of *soror*, means "a society of girls or women."

Most third declension abstract nouns like *vēritās* (truth), *cupiditās* (desire), *lībertās* (freedom), *pāx* (peace), and *virtūs* (manliness, courage) are feminine. *Virtūs* follows this pattern and is feminine even though its first syllable is *vir* (man). *Virtūs* is related to the English word "virtue," but it has quite a different connotation in Latin: *virtūs* implies not moral goodness but "aggressiveness or courage."

Another interesting third declension noun is *mōs, mōris* (m.), meaning "custom, moral." Caesar uses this word in *Dē Bellō Gallicō* when he is describing the local customs of the tribes he encounters in Gaul, Germany, and Britain. Of course, the English word "mores" (customs) is simply the plural of *mōs*, and is used exactly the same way by modern ethnographers or anthropologists.

As you master third declension nouns, you will often find that the English derivatives are especially useful in learning genitives. For example, "matriarch" (matron, materfamilias) is a reminder that the genitive of *māter* ends in –*tris*, not –*teris*. Similarly, "nepotism" (favoring a family member) tells you that the genitive of *nepōs* is *nepōtis*, and "regal" (royal) tells you to change the *x* of *rēx* to *g* for the genitive *rēgis*, just as "pacify" (make peace) tells you to change the *x* of *pāx* to *c* for the genitive *pācis*.

EXERCISES

I. Fill in the blank with the meaning of each English word. Some of the English meanings were discussed above, some may require a dictionary, and some you may know already or can guess.

Latin word	English word	Meaning of English
1. *amor, amōris* (m.) = love	amorous	_____
2. *labor, labōris* (m.) = labor	laborious	_____
3. *timor, timōris* (m.) = fear	timorous	_____
4. *uxor, uxōris* (f.) = wife	uxorious	_____
5. *soror, sorōris* (f.) = sister	sorority	_____
6. *pater, patris* (m.) = father	paternal	_____
7. *māter, mātris* (f.) = mother	matriarch	_____
8. *frāter, frātris* (m.) = brother	fratricide	_____
9. *rēx, rēgis* (m.) = king	regicide	_____
10. *mōs, mōris* (m.) = habit, custom	mores	_____
11. *nepōs, nepōtis* (m.) = grandson, descendant	nepotism	_____
12. *homō, hominis* (m.) = human being	homage	_____
13. *cīvis, cīvis* (c.) = citizen	civic	_____
14. *virtūs, virtūtis* (f.) = manliness, courage	virtuoso	_____
15. *cīvitās, cīvitātis* (f.) = state, citizenship	city	_____
16. *lībertās, lībertātis* (f.) = freedom	liberty	_____
17. *vēritās, vēritātis* (f.) = truth	verity	_____
18. *cupiditās, cupiditātis* (f.) = desire	cupidity	_____
19. *celeritās, celeritātis* (f.) = speed	accelerate	_____
20. *pāx, pācis* (f.) = peace	pacify	_____

21. *urbs, urbis* (f.) = city   urban   _____

                             urbane   _____

22. *vōx, vōcis* (f.) = voice   advocate   _____

                             equivocal   _____

23. *prex, precis* (f.) = prayer, request   deprecate   _____

                             precarious   _____

24. *crux, crucis* (f.) = cross   crux   _____

                             crucial   _____

II. Translate.

1. pax vobiscum   _____

2. Pax Romana   _____

3. homo sapiens   _____

4. ad hominem   _____

5. labor omnia vincit   _____

6. civis Romanus sum   _____

7. dona nobis pacem   _____

8. urbs aeterna   _____

III. Match the Latin word with its English meaning.

1. _____ *mōs*   A. human being

2. _____ *vēritās*   B. manliness, courage

3. _____ *virtūs*   C. custom, habit

4. _____ *cupiditās*   D. state, citizenship

5. _____ *cīvitās*   E. truth

6. _____ *timor*   F. wife

7. _____ *lībertās*   G. fear

8. _____ *homō*   H. desire

9. _____ *uxor*   I. freedom

10. _____ *pāx*   J. peace

IV. Choose and circle the best answer from A, B, C, or D.

1. According to legend, Romulus was guilty of

    A. regicide   B. fratricide

    C. tyrannicide   D. infanticide

2. A husband who always does what his wife wants might be described as

    A. censorious   B. mendacious

    C. uxorious   D. contentious

3. The English word **nepotism** is derived from the Latin word for

    A. grandson   B. uncle

    C. grandparent   D. aunt

4. Members of a **sorority** are expected to treat each other like

    A. rivals   B. acquaintances

    C. business associates   D. sisters

5. Ancient Roman society can be described as

    A. utopian   B. plebeian

    C. matriarchal   D. patriarchal

V. Answer briefly. NB: you may need to use a dictionary or an Internet site.

1. What does the phrase *ad hominem* mean in a modern political context? Give an example of the kind of accusation that would constitute an *ad hominem* attack.

    _____

    _____

2. What was the Pax Romana?

    _____

3. The poet Ovid was probably remembering the phrase *"Labor omnia vincit"* when he wrote *"Amor omnia vincit."* Translate both phrases.

    _____

    _____

4. Name the dinosaur whose name implies that he was a "king."

    _____

5. Define the following words.

    matricide   _____

    patricide   _____

    homicide   _____

    suicide   _____

    pesticide   _____

CHAPTER 18
THIRD DECLENSION NEUTER NOUN DERIVATIVES

Third declension neuter nouns do not follow any particular pattern in the nominative singular. This makes them a troublesome lot, especially compared with their second declension counterparts that are so easily recognizable by the almost invariable *–um* ending in the nominative singular. Some third declension neuters have nominatives ending in *–men*. Words like *lūmen, līmen, nōmen, nūmen, flūmen,* and *fulmen* are examples of this group. Other third declension neuters like *corpus, latus, foedus, opus, onus, genus, pectus,* and *tempus* have nominatives ending in *–us*. But some neuters like *iter* and *caput* don't belong to either of these groups.

Genitives can also be a challenge for this group of nouns. Why, for instance, does *lūmen* change to *lūminis* while the genitive of *iter* is *itineris*? Why do *corpus* and *tempus* add the syllable *–or* when they change to *corporis* and *temporis* in the genitive? It is here that derivatives can be helpful. If, for example, you know that "luminous" (full of light, bright) is a derivative of *lūmen,* it is easy to remember the genitive *lūminis* and thus the base *lūmin–.* Plus, you can see that *lūmen* must have something to do with light. Similarly, "itinerary" (plan for a journey), "corporal" (bodily), and "temporary" (for a short time) can all serve as helpful reminders of the base of each neuter noun: *itiner–* for *iter, corpor–* for *corpus,* and *tempor–* for *tempus.*

Sometimes, a derivative will help you distinguish between a neuter noun like *latus, -eris* (side) and a look-alike word such as the adjective *lātus, -a, -um* (wide). Words like "multilateral" (many sided) and "unilateral" (one sided) are reminders of the genitive *lateris* and could never have anything to do with width. Equally, "flume" (a channel containing a swift-flowing stream) and "fulminate" (explode, detonate) are useful in differentiating between *flūmen,* which means "stream or river," and *fulmen,* which means "a lightning bolt."

Sometimes, a derivative is a helpful reminder of a Latin preposition. The prefix *ex* in "expectorate" (spit out), for example, tells you that "out" will be part of the English word's definition. The prefix *dē* in "decapitate" (behead) reminds you that something is falling down! Similarly, the prefix *sub* in "subliminal" (below the threshold of consciousness) prompts you to recognize that something "under or below" is involved. Finally, some Latin neuter nouns come directly into English. In both languages an "onus" is "a burden," "opus" is "a work," and "genus" is "a kind or sort."

EXERCISES

I. Fill in the blank with the meaning of each English word. Some of the English meanings were discussed above, some may require a dictionary, and some you may know already or can guess.

	Latin word	*English word*	*Meaning of English*
1.	*līmen, līminis* (n.) = threshold	subliminal	_____
2.	*lūmen, lūminis* (n.) = light, eye	luminous	_____
		luminary	_____
3.	*flūmen, flūminis* (n.) = river, stream	flume	_____
4.	*fulmen, fulminis* (n.) = lightning bolt	fulminate	_____
5.	*nōmen, nōminis* (n.) = name	nominate	_____
		nominative	_____
		nominal	_____
6.	*nūmen, nūminis* (n.) = divine will, deity	numinous	_____
7.	*corpus, corporis* (n.) = body	corporal	_____
8.	*caput, capitis* (n.) = head	decapitate	_____
9.	*latus, lateris* (n.) = side	multilateral	_____
10.	*foedus, foederis* (n.) = league, treaty	federation	_____
11.	*onus, oneris* (n.) = burden	onerous	_____
12.	*pectus, pectoris* (n.) = chest, heart	expectorate	_____
		pectoral	_____
13.	*tempus, temporis* (n.) = time	temporary	_____
14.	*mūnus, mūneris* (n.) = gift, reward	remunerate	_____

15. *vulnus, vulneris* (n.) = wound   vulnerable   _____

   invulnerable   _____

16. *opus, operis* (n.) = work   opus   _____

17. *genus, generis* (n.) = kind, sort   genus   _____

18. *iter, itineris* (n.) = route, journey   itinerary   _____

II.

Translate these phrases. NB: you may need to use a dictionary or an Internet site.

1. numen lumen (motto of the University of Wisconsin) _____
2. habeas corpus _____
3. tempus fugit _____
4. pro tempore _____
5. onus probandi _____
6. magnum opus _____
7. sui generis _____
8. corpus delicti _____

III.

Give the genitive for each noun.

1. fulmen, _____ (n.) = lightning bolt
2. genus, _____ (n.) = kind, sort
3. latus, _____ (n.) = side, flank
4. foedus, _____ (n.) = league, treaty
5. nūmen, _____ (n.) = divine will, deity
6. pectus, _____ (n.) = chest, heart
7. mūnus, _____ (n.) = gift, reward
8. onus, _____ (n.) = burden
9. flūmen, _____ (n.) = river

10. nūmen, _____ (n.) = divine will, deity

11. vulnus, _____ (n.) = wound

12. caput, _____ (n.) = head

13. nōmen, _____ (n.) = name

14. corpus, _____ (n.) = body

IV. Match the Latin word with its English meaning.

1. _____	*fulmen*	A.	route, journey
2. _____	*onus*	B.	river
3. _____	*iter*	C.	lightning bolt
4. _____	*foedus*	D.	burden
5. _____	*mūnus*	E.	name
6. _____	*latus, -eris*	F.	gift, reward
7. _____	*lūmen*	G.	side, flank
8. _____	*līmen*	H.	light
9. _____	*nōmen*	I.	league, treaty
10. _____	*nūmen*	J.	divine will, deity
11. _____	*flūmen*	K.	work
12. _____	*genus*	L.	head
13. _____	*caput*	M.	kind, sort
14. _____	*opus*	N.	chest, heart
15. _____	*pectus*	O.	threshold

V. Answer briefly. NB: you may need to use a dictionary or an Internet site.

1. Works of classical music are labeled with the abbreviation Op. plus a number. What Latin word does Op. stand for?

   _____

2. A *magnum opus* is a masterpiece. Why does *magnum* end in –*um*? (Hint: Remember the rule for agreement of adjectives in Latin.)

   _____

3. What does the legal term *habeas corpus* mean? Name the American president who suspended the right of *habeas corpus* during a time of national emergency.

   _____

4. What does the abbreviation *pro tem.* stand for? How do you translate the phrase? What is the primary function of the President Pro Tem. of the Senate? Who serves as President Pro Tem. of the Senate? Who is the current President Pro Tem. of the Senate?

   _____

   _____

   _____

5. The word "capital" in English is derived from the Latin word *caput, capitis*. What is the derivation of the English word "Capitol"? Use each word in an English sentence to show its meaning.

   _____

   _____

   _____

6. The Latin word for "knee" is *genū, genūs*. What declension does it belong to? How do you know?

   _____

7. The Latin verb *adnuere* means "to nod assent." What would it indicate when a divinity nodded assent? What is the neuter noun for "divine will, deity?"

   _____

8. *Iter, itineris* means "journey, route." What does the idiom *iter facere* mean?

   _____

9. You have probably heard of the Swedish botanist Linnaeus who devised a two-part system of identifying all living things by *genus* and *species*. What is this system of naming plants and animals called? (Hint: Both words are derivatives of the Latin word *nōmen, nōminis*.)

   _____

VI. Choose and circle the best answer from A, B, C, or D.

1. A *magnum opus* is

   A. a relict
   B. a masterpiece
   C. an innovation
   D. an imitation

2. The English words **nominative**, **nominal**, and **nominate** all come from the Latin word meaning

   A. noun
   B. appointment
   C. announcement
   D. name

3. The *Sēquana*, *Rhēnus*, *Rubicō*, and *Tiberis* are examples of

   A. *flūmina*
   B. *patriae*
   C. *prōvinciae*
   D. *itinera*

4. In preparing a case, a prosecuting attorney must consider the

   A. opus citatum
   B. tabula rasa
   C. corpus delicti
   D. post scriptum

5. The root word for the English words **illuminate**, **luminary**, and **luminous** is the Latin word for

   A. celebrity
   B. power
   C. speech
   D. light

CHAPTER 19
PRONOUN DERIVATIVES

"Quiddity," "quidnunc": where did these peculiar English words come from? What do they mean? The answer to the first question is: they come from Latin, of course! They are both derivatives of the Latin interrogative pronoun *quis, quid* (who, what). And the answer to the second question is: if you recognize the Latin root, you will not only know a new English word, but you will also have a way to remember an important Latin pronoun. "Quiddity" is "what creates the essential nature of something," and a "quidnunc" is "a gossip," i.e., someone who is always saying "what now? what now?"

The abbreviation *i.e.* stands for the Latin words *id est* (that is), and *id* is the neuter Latin personal pronoun that means "it." In psychology, the "id" is the part of the human psyche that is controlled by impulses. Another term in psychology, the "ego," is also a Latin pronoun. It refers to "a person's conscience." *Ego* (I) is the nominative of the Latin personal pronoun, and it is clearly the root of "egotism" (conceit, narcissism) and "egotistical" (self-centered). In addition, the English word "me" is both the accusative and ablative of *ego*. Here a Latin phrase used in English can be a useful reminder of a quirk of Latin grammar: *vāde mēcum* (an essential piece of equipment) literally means "go with me" and originally referred to "a manual or handbook." Notice the inversion of the Latin preposition *cum* and the ablative object *mē*. This reversal of the normal word order is found not only with *mē* but also with other personal pronouns like *tē, vōbīs,* and *nōbīs*. You can see it with the phrases *pāx vōbīscum* (peace be with you) and *pāx nōbīscum* (peace be with us).

Once you know the pronoun *is, ea, id*, it is easy to recognize the pronoun *īdem, eadem, idem* (the same). Queen Elizabeth I of England took the phrase *semper eadem* as her motto to emphasize her unchanging nature. Notice that the *ea–* of *eadem* is a form of *is* and *–dem* remains the same throughout the declension.

Along with *semper eadem*, other Latin phrases still used in English will help you remember other pronouns. *Ad hoc* (for this purpose) will remind you of the demonstrative pronoun *hic, haec, hoc* (this). Another phrase, *post hoc ergō propter hoc* (after this therefore because of this) means that when one event follows another, there is a causal relationship between the two happenings. Both phrases are reminders that *hoc* is neuter, and that all three prepositions, *ad* (to), *post* (after), and *propter* (because) take the accusative.

Finally, the abbreviated phrase *et al.* (and the others) is probably familiar to you if you have ever seen an entry in a bibliography for an article or book with several authors. This abbreviation is also found in the names of court cases when there are multiple parties involved. For example, if several people file a suit together as a group, the case might be listed as Jones v. Smith, et al. *Et al.* stands for *et aliī* (and the others). *Aliī* comes from the pronoun *alius, alia, aliud* (other), which is the root of the English words "alias" and "alibi."

EXERCISES

I. Fill in the blank with the meaning of each English word. Some of the English meanings were discussed above, some may require a dictionary, and some you may know already or can guess.

Latin word	English word or phrase	Meaning of English
1. *quis, quid* = who, what	quiddity	_____
	quidnunc	_____
	quid pro quo	_____
2. *quī, quae, quod* = who, which	quorum	_____
3. *alius, alia, aliud* = other	alias	_____
	alibi	_____
	et alii, et alia	_____
4. *is, ea, id* = he, she, it	id	_____
	id est	_____
5. *īdem, eadem, idem* = the same	semper eadem	_____
6. *hic, haec, hoc* = this	ad hoc	_____
7. *ego, meī* = I	ego	_____
	egotistical	_____
	egotism	_____
	vade mecum	_____
8. *nōs* = we	pax nobiscum	_____
9. *vōs* = you	pax vobiscum	_____

II. Fill in the blanks with a Latin phrase.

1. At our last meeting our club was unable to vote on a proposal because we did not have a _____ (number of members of a group required to be present to transact business).

2. One teacher will serve on the _____ (for this purpose) committee for publicity.

3. The recent alumni, _____ (that is) the graduates of the last five years, will attend a reunion this spring.

4. The priest ended the service with the words _____ (peace be with you).

5. If I help you with math, and you help me with Latin, will you consider it _____ (tit for tat)?

III. Match the derivative with its meaning.

1. _____ alibi
2. _____ quiddity
3. _____ alias
4. _____ quidnunc
5. _____ egotistical
6. _____ quorum

A. self-centered
B. required number for a valid vote
C. essential nature
D. assumed name
E. gossip
F. defense of being elsewhere

IV. Give the meanings of these Latin pronouns.

1. quī, quae, quod _____
2. quis, quid _____
3. is, ea, id _____
4. hic, haec, hoc _____
5. īdem, eadem, idem _____
6. ego _____
7. nōs _____
8. tū _____
9. vōs _____
10. alius, alia, aliud _____

V. Answer briefly.

1. What case is *quōrum*? _____
2. What case is *hoc* when it is the object of *ad* or *propter*? _____
3. What case is *mē* when it is the object of *cum*? _____
4. What is the nominative of *mē*? _____
5. Write in Latin.

   with you (plural) _____

   with us _____

CHAPTER 20
FIRST AND SECOND CONJUGATION VERB DERIVATIVES

Have you ever worked on a science project that required you to keep track of the data? Or, have you ever noticed a list of errata at the end of an article you were reading? Both "data" and "errata" are English words derived from Latin verbs. "Data" comes from the verb *dō, dare, dedī, datum* (give), and it means "facts or statistics that are given." "Errata" comes from *errō, errāre, errāvī, errātum* (wander, make a mistake), and it means "a list of errors." Both "data" and "errata" are plural. The singular of "data" is "datum," and the singular of "errata" is "erratum," but the singulars are not used very often in English. Remember, you have already encountered "datum" in chapter 16.

Dō, dare, dedī, datum and *errō, errāre, errāvī, errātum* both belong to the same conjugation of Latin verbs. A conjugation is a group of verbs that share stems and endings. All the verbs in the same conjugation follow the same pattern. The word "conjugation" comes from the Latin verb *iungō* that means "to join." *Dō, errō, ambulō, pugnō*, and other verbs with the ending *–āre* in the second principal part are "joined together" in the group known as first conjugation. Verbs like *videō* and *moneō* with the ending *–ēre* in the second principal part belong to the second group or conjugation.

Derivatives are always a good way to tell the difference between similar-sounding verbs of any conjugation. For example, if you know that the English word "conserve" means "save," it will be easy to remember that *servō* (preserve, keep, guard) is not the same as the fourth conjugation *serviō* (serve, be a slave to). Similarly, you will be able to distinguish *maneō* (stay, remain) from *moneō* (warn, advise) if you think of "permanent" (remaining forever) and "premonition" (a forewarning).

In addition, derivatives can prompt you when you are having trouble remembering a particular grammatical term. For instance, when you know that "imperative" (the command form of a verb) comes from *imperō* (command), you will never confuse it with the "vocative" (noun of direct address) that is derived from *vocō* (call). And since you know that the root of the word "dative" is the verb *dō, dare, dedī, datum* (give), it will be easy to remember that the dative case is often found as the ending for people to whom something is given.

EXERCISES

I. Fill in the blank with the meaning of each English word. Some of the English meanings were discussed above, some may require a dictionary, and some you may know already or can guess.
NB: The first conjugation verbs marked with (1) have principal parts following the pattern *–āre, –āvī, –ātum*. Only a few like *stō, dō, iuvō,* and *vetō* fail to follow the pattern; all principal parts of these first conjugation verbs are listed.

	Latin word	English word	Meaning of English
1.	*amō* (1) = love, like	amateur	_____
		amity	_____
2.	*errō* (1) = wander, make a mistake	error	_____
		erratum, errata	_____
3.	*ambulō* (1) = walk	ambulatory	_____
4.	*pugnō* (1) = fight	pugilist	_____
		pugnacious	_____
		repugnant	_____
5.	*vocō* (1) = call	vocative	_____
		vocation	_____
6.	*imperō* (1) = command	imperative	_____
7.	*parō* (1) = prepare	prepare	_____
8.	*laudō* (1) = praise	laudable	_____
9.	*servō* (1) = keep, save	conserve	_____
10.	*superō* (1) = surpass, conquer	insuperable	_____
11.	*vulnerō* (1) = wound	invulnerable	_____
12.	*dō, dare, dedī, datum* = give	datum, data	_____
13.	*iuvō, iuvāre, iūvī, iūtum* = help	adjutant	_____
14.	*stō, stāre, stetī, statum* = stand	status	_____
15.	*habitō* (1) = live in, dwell	habitat	_____

16. *dēbeō, -ēre, dēbuī, dēbitum*
    = owe, ought   debt   _____

17. *moneō, -ēre, monuī,*
    monitum = warn,   premonition   _____
    advise

18. *maneō, -ēre, mānsī,*
    mānsum = stay,   permanent   _____
    remain

19. *rīdeō, -ēre, rīsī, rīsum*
    = laugh   deride   _____

20. *videō, -ēre, vīdī, vīsum*
    = see   visible   _____

II. Translate.

1. errare humanum est   _____

2. status quo   _____

3. videre est credere   _____

III. Match the Latin word with its English meaning.

1. _____ *laudō*   A. stay, remain
2. _____ *iuvō*   B. give
3. _____ *moneō*   C. prepare
4. _____ *servō*   D. praise
5. _____ *habitō*   E. warn, advise
6. _____ *videō*   F. help
7. _____ *dō*   G. live in, dwell
8. _____ *parō*   H. see
9. _____ *maneō*   I. keep, save
10. _____ *stō*   J. stand

IV.

Choose and circle the best answer from A, B, C, or D.

1. The words **advocate**, **vocation**, and **provoke** all come from the Latin verb that means

   A. defend   B. promote

   C. call   D. irritate

2. If a coach **lauds** a player's moves, the coach is

   A. praising the player   B. scolding the player

   C. advising the player   D. excusing the player

3. **Premonition**, **admonish**, and **monitor** are derived from the Latin verb that means

   A. remain   B. observe

   C. worry   D. warn

4. It is clear from the Latin root of the word that an **adjutant** is expected to be

   A. alert   B. omniscient

   C. helpful   D. watchful

5. Which English word does **not** come from the Latin verb *servō, servāre*?

   A. preserve   B. conserve

   C. servile   D. observe

V.

Answer briefly. NB: you may need to use a dictionary or an Internet site.

1. "Cum laude" means "with praise." Translate "magna cum laude" and "summa cum laude."

   _____

2. Name the famous Roman who wrote "*Vēnī, vīdī, vīcī*" after a victory in battle. Translate the phrase.

   _____

3. What modern organization has the Latin motto "semper paratus?" What does this motto mean? What Latin verb does *parātus* come from? The Marines have a similar Latin motto. Give the Marine motto in Latin and in English.

   _____

   _____

4. Give the principal parts and meanings of *stō, dō, iuvō,* and *vetō.*

    _____

    _____

5. Make a list of as many English derivatives as possible from the Latin verb *videō, vidēre, vīdī, vīsum.*
    Hint: Think of prefixes like *pro–, e–, re–* and endings like *–ent, –al, –ion,* and remember to think about
    English words that come from the fourth principal part *vīsum.*

    _____

    _____

    _____

    _____

6. Look at the group of English words below. Use a Latin dictionary to find the first principal part and
    meaning of the verb from which each word comes. Then, use an English dictionary to find the defini-
    tion of each word as an English noun.

	Latin root verb	*Translation of root verb*	*English meaning*
caret	_____	_____	_____
caveat	_____	_____	_____
delete	_____	_____	_____
placebo	_____	_____	_____
tenet	_____	_____	_____
ignoramus	_____	_____	_____

CHAPTER 21
THIRD AND FOURTH CONJUGATION AND IRREGULAR VERB DERIVATIVES

While the principal parts of first and second conjugation verbs often follow a predictable pattern, the principal parts of other verbs are much more variable. For instance, the irregular verb *ferō, ferre* (bear, carry, say, tell) changes to *tulī, lātum* in its third and fourth principal parts. Fortunately, a variety of English derivatives can be of help here. "Refer," "relate," "transfer," and "translate" all are derivatives of *ferō*. These English words are familiar so the challenge is simply connecting the relevant derivative to the right part of the verb.

Once you have mastered *ferō*, the last two principal parts of *tollō* (raise, lift, steal) are easy because you can see that both *sustulī* and *sublātum* are related to *tulī, lātum*. And for the first two principal parts of *tollō*, a derivative will again provide help: "extol" means "exalt or lift up in praise."

The irregular verb *sum, esse, fuī, futūrus* (be) is another challenge because its principal parts are so different that they do not seem to belong to the same verb. But, once again, a derivative can help. Think of the English word "essence" (core of being), and you can remember that *esse* is the infinitive of *sum*. "Futuristic" (of or pertaining to the future) will remind you that *futūrus* is the fourth principal part of *sum*.

Even a regular verb like *pōnō, pōnere, posuī, positum* (put, place) can pose problems unless you remember more than one derivative. Here, "proponent" (an advocate or supporter) and "position" (place) are useful reminders of the first and fourth principal parts of the verb. Similarly, "tangent" (a line that touches a curve) and "tactile" (having to do with the sense of touch) will help you recall the first and last principal parts of the verb *tangō, tangere, tetigī, tāctum* (touch). In the same way, "revolve" (turn around, rotate) and "revolution" (revolt, uprising) are useful in remembering those principal parts of the verb *volvō, volvere, volvī, volūtum* (turn, roll, unwind). *Volvere* can mean "think about something by turning it over in thought." It can also mean "roll or unroll a scroll," and the English word "volume" is derived from *volūmen*, the Latin word for a scroll. Of course, you might simply remember the first part of *volvō* if you think about a brand of car whose name means, "I roll"!

Finally, you may have wondered why English words like "proceed" (go forward) and "procession" (parade), while clearly related, are not spelled in the same way. These derivatives, therefore, will help you learn the principal parts of *cēdō, cēdere, cessī, cessum* (go, yield), and at the same time a quirk in English spelling.

EXERCISES

I. Fill in the blank with the meaning of each English word. Some of the English meanings were discussed above, some may require a dictionary, and some you may know already or can guess.

Latin word	*English word*	*Meaning of English*
1. *agō, agere, ēgī, actum* = do, drive	agent	_____
	actor	_____
	agenda	_____
2. *audiō, -īre, -īvī, -ītum* = hear, listen	audible	_____
	audition	_____
3. *capiō, -ere, cēpī, captum* = take, capture	captive	_____
4. *cēdō, cēdere, cessī, cessum* = go, yield	proceed	_____
	procession	_____
	secede	_____
5. *crēdō, crēdere, crēdidī, crēditum* = believe	credit	_____
6. *dīcō, dīcere, dīxī, dictum* = say, tell	dictate	_____
7. *faciō, facere, fēcī, factum* = do, make	factory	_____
8. *frangō, -ere, frēgī, frāctum* = break, wreck	fraction	_____
	frangible	_____
9. *petō, petere, petīvī, petītum* = seek, beg	compete	_____
	petition	_____
	centripetal	_____
10. *pōnō, pōnere, posuī, positum* = put, place	proponent	_____
	deposit	_____

11. *regō, regere, rēxī, rēctum*   regal   _____
    = rule

                                        insurrection _____

12. *relinquō, -ere, relīquī,*   reliquary   _____
    relictum = abandon,
    leave behind

                                        derelict   _____

13. *sentiō, sentīre, sēnsī,*   sentient   _____
    sēnsum = feel

                                        sensitive   _____

14. *tangō, tangere, tetigī,*   tangent   _____
    tāctum = touch

                                        tactile   _____

15. *tollō, tollere, sustulī,*   extol   _____
    sublātum = lift, exalt

16. *volvō, volvere, volvī,*   revolve   _____
    volūtum = roll

                                        revolution   _____

17. *sum, esse, fuī, futūrus* = be   essence   _____

                                        futuristic   _____

18. *possum, posse, potuī* = be   posse   _____
    able

                                        potential   _____

19. *ferō, ferre, tulī, lātum* =   transfer   _____
    bear, carry, say

                                        translation   _____

20. *eō, īre, īvī, itum* = go   exit   _____

21. *volō, velle, voluī* = want,   volition   _____
    wish

22. *nōlō, nōlle, nōluī* = be   nolo contendere _____
    unwilling

II. Translate.

1. nolens, volens _____

2. noli me tangere! _____

3. exeunt omnes _____

III.
Make a flash card for each verb in exercise I. Write the Latin on one side and the English meaning on the other. Use a different color of ink to add derivatives that you find useful.

IV.
Give the first two principal parts of the Latin verb from which each English word is derived.

1. captivate, captor _____

2. agent, actor _____

3. essence _____

4. petition, compete _____

5. exponent, position _____

6. proceed, procession, secede, secession _____

7. tangent, tactful _____

8. relinquish, relict _____

9. benevolent _____

10. refer, transfer, relate, translate _____

11. transit, exit, transient _____

12. extol _____

13. credit _____

V.

Match the Latin word with its English meaning.

1. _____ *nōlō*
2. _____ *possum*
3. _____ *dīcō*
4. _____ *petō*
5. _____ *pōnō*
6. _____ *agō*
7. _____ *regō*
8. _____ *cēdō*
9. _____ *volvō*
10. _____ *relinquō*

A. leave behind, abandon
B. go, yield
C. do, drive
D. roll, wind, turn over in the mind
E. seek, beg, attack
F. rule
G. say, tell
H. be able
I. be unwilling
J. put, place

VI.

Test yourself by giving the missing principal part and the meaning of each Latin verb.

1. agō, agere, ēgī, _____   _____

2. audiō, _____, audīvī, audītum   _____

3. capiō, _____, cēpī, captum   _____

4. cēdō, cēdere, cessī, _____   _____

5. crēdō, crēdere, crēdidī, _____   _____

6. dīcō, dīcere, dīxī, _____   _____

7. faciō, _____, fēcī, factum   _____

8. petō, petere, petīvī, _____   _____

9. pōnō, pōnere, posuī, _____   _____

10. regō, regere, rēxī, _____   _____

11. relinquō, relinquere, relīquī, _____   _____

12. sentiō, sentīre, sēnsī, _____   _____

13. tangō, tangere, tetigī, _____   _____

14. tollō, tollere, sustulī, _____   _____

15. volvō, volvere, volvī, _____   _____

16. sum, esse, fuī, _____   _____

17. possum, posse, _____   _____

18. ferō, ferre, tulī, _____   _____

19. eō, īre, īvī, _____   _____

20. volō, velle, _____   _____

21. nōlō, nōlle, _____   _____

VII. Choose and circle the best answer from A, B, C, or D.

1. **Secede** and **secession** are derivatives of the Latin verb that means

    A. go   B. fall

    C. cut   D. meet

2. **Compete**, **petition**, and **appetite** are derivatives of the Latin verb that means

    A. rival   B. yield

    C. eat   D. seek

3. In court a plea of *nolo contendere* means that the defendant accepts penalty as if guilty but does not want to

    A. go to trial   B. pay bail

    C. hire a lawyer   D. have the trial date changed

4. **Exit**, **transit**, and **transient** are derivatives of the Latin verb

    A. *emō*   B. *iaciō*

    C. *eō*   D. *ferō*

5. A **relict** is something that has been

    A. stolen   B. left behind

    C. sought after   D. believed in

CHAPTER 22
DEPONENT VERB DERIVATIVES

As a Latin student you know that the Latin preposition *dē* means "down from," and that the Latin verb *pōnō* means "put or place." Think of the two words together and you can easily remember that the term "deponent" refers to a group of quirky Latin verbs that have "put down" their active forms. Deponent verbs are passive in form, but they are active in meaning. One way to understand deponents is to think about the English equivalent of the Latin deponent verb *nāscor* (be born). The English "be born," just like the Latin *nāscor*, is neither completely active nor entirely passive.

Deponents are a rich source of interesting English derivatives. Think about all the English words related to *loquor*, the deponent that means "speak." It is obviously the root of English words like "eloquent" (well spoken) and "elocution" (the art of public speaking). *Loquor* also gives us words like "colloquial," which means "informal speech," and "colloquium," which means "a meeting that involves discussion." "Soliloquy" is another interesting English word with *loquor* at its root. You might assume that the word "soliloquy" is a synonym for "monologue" (a speech given by a single person). But if you know that the prefix *sōli–* means "alone," you will quickly realize that a "soliloquy" is indeed "a speech by a single person, but that person must be alone." When delivered on stage, a "soliloquy" allows the audience to know what a person is thinking as the speaker is addressing him- or herself. A "monologue," on the other hand, is "a speech by one actor or performer addressed to listeners, either fellow actors on stage or members of an audience."

As always, a good way to remember the meaning of Latin deponents is to make a connection between the deponent and a familiar English word derived from it. For example, *arbitror* gives us English words like "arbitrator" (someone who makes a judgment call in a dispute) and "arbitration" (settling a disagreement by means of a discussion in which the participants are expected to abide by the decision of an arbitrator). Both "arbitrator" and "arbitration" will help you remember that *arbitror* means "judge."

Sometimes the evolution of an English derivative provides an interesting twist that makes it easy to learn the Latin root word. For instance, *hortor* in Latin means "urge, encourage," and a "cohort" in the army of ancient Rome was "a small group within a legion." Members of a cohort encouraged and supported each other. A "cohort" today in English means "a companion, someone who encourages and urges a friend to persevere."

Deponents show up in a number of Latin phrases that are still found in English, and knowing a particular phrase can often fix the meaning of a certain deponent in your memory. Perhaps you are finding that the Latin word *labor* is tricky because it can be a noun meaning "work" or it can be a deponent verb meaning "slip or glide." To learn the deponent verb *lābor*, it can be helpful to remember a phrase like *lāpsus memoriae* (a slip of the memory), *lāpsus pennae* (a slip of the pen), or *lāpsus linguae* (a slip of the tongue). Note also that the verb has a macron while the noun does not.

Similarly, the deponents *moror* (delay) and *morior* (die) are easily confused. Here, a phrase like *mementō morī*, a reminder of human mortality, is a good way to remember that the infinitive of *morior* is *morī* and that *morior* (whose infinitive is *morārī*) does not mean to delay. Another Latin phrase you may have encountered in English is a quotation from the poet Horace: *dulce et decorum est prō patriā morī*. The phrase means, "It is sweet and fitting to die for one's country," and the English poet Wilfred Owen used these words ironically as the title of a poem about the realities of trench warfare during World War I. Yet another phrase from *morior* is the cry of Roman gladiators, *"Moritūrī tē salūtāmus!"* (We about to die salute you!).

Deponents are a vital part of Latin vocabulary. So, whether you use a derivative or a whole phrase as an aid, it is an important group to master.

EXERCISES

I. Fill in the blank with the meaning of each English word. Some of the English meanings were discussed above, some may require a dictionary, and some you may know already or can guess.

Latin word	English word	Meaning of English
1. *arbitror, arbitrārī, arbitrātus* = judge	arbitrator	_____
2. *for, fārī, fātus* = say, foretell	affable	_____
	ineffable	_____
3. *hortor, hortārī, hortātus* = urge	cohort	_____
	exhort	_____
4. *moror, morārī, morātus* = delay	moratorium	_____
5. *vereor, verērī, veritus* = fear	reverence	_____
6. *loquor, loquī, locūtus* = speak	loquacious	_____
	soliloquy	_____
	colloquial	_____
	elocution	_____
7. *lābor, lābī, lāpsus* = slip, glide	elapse	_____
8. *sequor, sequī, secūtus* = follow	sequel	_____

9. *nāscor, nāscī, nātus* = be born   neonatal _____

                prenatal _____

10. *ūtor, ūtī, ūsus* = use   usury _____

11. *morior, morī, mortuus* = die   mortuary _____

12. *patior, patī, passus* = suffer, allow   patient _____

                passion _____

II. Translate these phrases. NB: you may need to use a dictionary or an Internet site.

1. lapsus pennae _____
2. lapsus memoriae _____
3. lapsus linguae _____
4. non sequitur _____
5. res ipsa loquitur _____
6. dulce et decorum est pro patria mori _____
7. morituri te salutamus _____
8. memento mori _____

III. Match the derivative with its English meaning.

1. _____ cohort   A. delay
2. _____ exhort   B. companion
3. _____ neonatal   C. slip of the tongue
4. _____ moratorium   D. urge, encourage
5. _____ arbitrator   E. talkative
6. _____ loquacious   F. newborn
7. _____ lapsus linguae   G. judge, referee
8. _____ usury   H. slip by
9. _____ elapse   I. a high rate of interest
10. _____ colloquium   J. meeting involving discussion

IV. Answer briefly. NB: you may need to use a dictionary or an Internet site.

1. *Res ipsa loquitur* means "the thing speaks for itself." When would someone say this phrase? What would be the tone of the person who says it? Describe an exchange in which the phrase might be appropriate.

   _____

   _____

   _____

2. The Renaissance is the period of European history that follows the Middle Ages. During the Renaissance, authors and artists were inspired by works of antiquity, and interest in the world of ancient Greece and Rome was reborn. Another way to spell Renaissance is Renascence. What Latin deponent verb is the root of Renascence and what is the meaning of the root word?

   _____

3. If a lending institution is accused of "usury," what is its alleged crime?

   _____

4. The prefix *in–* sometimes means "not." What is the root of the English word "infant"? (Hint: What is an infant unable to do?)

   _____

V. Choose and circle the best answer from A, B, C, or D.

1. The English words **patient** and **passion** both come from the Latin verb that means

   A. suffer, allow B. slip, glide

   C. urge, encourage D. judge, think

2. The English word **moratorium** is derived from the Latin word

   A. *morior* B. *moror*

   C. *mors* D. *morbus*

3. An **arbitrator** is someone who is skilled as

   A. a referee B. an architect

   C. an actor D. a banker

4. The deponent verb *loquor* is similar in meaning to

   A. *moneō* B. *dīcō*

   C. *laudō* D. *audiō*

5. **Sequel**, **sequence**, **consequence**, and **consecutive** are all derived from the Latin word that means

    A. prefigure   B. succeed

    C. execute   D. follow

6. **Prenatal** and **neonatal** are derivatives of the Latin deponent that means to

    A. become   B. nurture

    C. be born   D. be made

7. The deponent verb *lābor* means

    A. work   B. yield

    C. collect   D. slip

8. Teachers often **exhort** their students to do their best. What does **exhort** mean?

    A. encourage   B. scold

    C. praise   D. endeavor

9. The term **deponent** is related to the verb

    A. *possum*   B. *putō*

    C. *pōnō*   D. *porrigō*

10. A drinking cup with images of a skeleton or a mosaic floor depicting a skeleton's head can be described as a

    A. *mementō morī*   B. *lāpsus memoriae*

    C. *nōn sequitur*   D. *rāra avis*

VI. Fill in the blanks for the principal parts of these deponents.

1. slip, glide = lābor, _____, lāpsus

2. suffer, allow = _____, patī, passus

3. die = morior, _____, mortuus

4. delay = _____, morārī, morātus

5. be born = _____, nāscī, nātus

6. use = ūtor, _____, ūsus

7. follow = sequor, sequī, _____

8. speak = loquor, loquī, _____

9. fear = vereor, _____, veritus

10. urge, encourage = hortor, _____, hortātus

11. say, foretell = for, fārī, _____

CHAPTER 23
ADJECTIVE DERIVATIVES

The English word "adjective" is derived from the Latin verb *iaciō, iacere, iēcī, iactum* (throw). And, of course, the first syllable of the word "adjective" is the Latin preposition *ad* meaning "to or toward." Thus, an adjective is literally a word thrown at a noun or pronoun to change or modify its meaning.

Latin adjectives, like Latin nouns, have case endings. Latin adjectives, however, have endings of all three genders because they must agree in gender, number, and case with the words they modify. Adjectives like *bonus, -a, -um* (good) or *līber, lībera, līberum* (free) have first and second declension endings. Other adjectives like *celer, celeris, celere* (swift) or *fortis, forte* (brave, strong) have third declension endings.

You will find English derivatives helpful as you work with Latin adjectives of both groups. For example, the English word "altitude" (elevation) will help you recall that *altus, -a, -um* means "high or deep," the English word "liberty" (freedom) will help you remember that *līber, lībera, līberum* means "free," and the English word "latitude" (width) will remind you of the difference between *laetus, -a, -um* (joyful) and *lātus, -a, -um* (wide). Sometimes, you can even see two Latin words in one English adjective. "Verisimilitude," which means "the appearance of truth," comes from a combination of *vērus, -a, -um* (true) and *similis, -e* (similar to), while "omnipotent," which means "all powerful," comes from *omnis, -e* (all) plus *potēns, -ntis* (powerful).

Of course, there are no familiar English derivatives for some adjectives like *ingēns* (huge). "Ingent" is an English word meaning "large," but it is rare. Furthermore, some Latin adjectives like *clārus, -a, -um* have several meanings. The English word "clarify" may help you remember the first two meanings of *clārus, -a, -um* (clear, bright), but not the other meaning (famous).

In both English and Latin, an adjective standing alone, without a noun to modify, sometimes functions as a noun. For example, in the English saying, "The good die young," clearly "good" stands for "good people." In this example, the adjective "good," which understands or replaces a noun, is called a substantive, and the reader must supply the implied noun. *Malus*, therefore, can mean "a bad man" while *ferus* is often translated as "a wild animal."

Personal possessive adjectives like *meus, mea, meum* (my) and *noster, nostra, nostrum* (our) present another challenge. These adjectives agree in gender, number, and case with the words they modify, so the possessor's gender is irrelevant. Here, a Latin phrase found in English usage today can be a helpful reminder of the way possessive adjectives work. For example, in the phrase *mea culpa* (my fault) the adjective *mea* is feminine because *culpa* is feminine, not because the speaker is necessarily a girl or a woman.

Finally, it is important to note that the dictionary form of an adjective in both English and Latin is called the positive degree. *Lātus* (wide) is an example of an adjective in the positive degree. To compare the width of two fields in English, however, you would say that one is "wider" than the other. "Wider" is the English comparative. In Latin the comparative of *lātus* is *lātior*. The superlative degree is *lātissimus* in Latin, "widest" in English. And here again derivatives can be helpful, especially when a Latin comparative or superlative does not seem to resemble the positive. For instance, if you know that *peior* (worse) is the root of the English word "pejorative" (negative, disparaging), you can see its connection to *malus* (bad). "Ameliorate" (make better) is a similar reminder that *melior* (better) is the comparative of *bonus* (good).

EXERCISES

I. Fill in the blank with the meaning of each English word. Some of the English meanings were discussed above, some may require a dictionary, and some you may know already or can guess.

	Latin word	*English word*	*Meaning of English*
1.	*magnus, -a, -um* = large, great	magnitude	_____
2.	*multus, -a, -um* = much, many	multitude	_____
3.	*malus, -a, -um* = bad, evil	malediction	_____
4.	*bonus, -a, -um* = good	bonus	_____
5.	*lātus, -a, -um* = wide	latitude	_____
6.	*altus, -a, -um* = high, deep; sea	altitude	_____
		exalt	_____
		alto	_____
7.	*ferus, -a, -um* = wild, wild animal	feral	_____
8.	*bellus, -a, -um* = beautiful	embellish	_____
		belle	_____
9.	*vērus, -a, -um* = true	verify	_____
		verisimilitude	_____
10.	*nullus, -a, -um* = no, none	nullify	_____
11.	*aequus, -a, -um* = equal	equity	_____
12.	*pulcher, -chra, -chrum* = beautiful	pulchritude	_____
13.	*miser, misera, miserum* = wretched	commiserate	_____
14.	*līber, lībera, līberum* = free	liberty	_____

15. *ācer, ācris, ācre* = sharp, bitter   acrimonious   _____

      acrid   _____

16. *celer, celeris, celere* = fast, swift   accelerate   _____

17. *omnis, omne* = all, every   omnibus   _____

      omniscient   _____

18. *fortis, forte* = brave, strong   fortitude   _____

19. *facilis, facile* = easy   facility   _____

20. *potēns, potentis* = powerful   omnipotent   _____

21. *similis, simile* = like   simile   _____

22. *vetus, veteris* = old   veteran   _____

      inveterate   _____

23. *dīligēns, dīligentis* = careful   diligent   _____

II.

A. Fill in the blank with the meaning of each English word. Some of the English meanings were discussed above, some may require a dictionary, and some you may know already or can guess.

Latin comparative	*English word*	*Meaning of English*
1. *melior, melius* = better	ameliorate	_____
2. *peior, peius* = worse	pejorative	_____
3. *maior, maius* = greater	major	_____
4. *minor, minus* = smaller	minor	_____
	minus	_____

Latin superlative	*English word*	*Meaning of English*
1. *optimus, -a, -um* = best	optimist	_____
2. *pessimus, -a, -um* = worst	pessimist	_____
3. *maximus, -a, -um* = greatest	maximum	_____
4. *minimus, -a, -um* = smallest	minimum	_____

B. Fill in the blank with the meaning of each phrase.

1. *meus, mea, meum* = my   mea culpa   _____

2. *noster, nostra, nostrum* = our   Pater Noster   _____

III.

Answer briefly. For some of the questions you may need to use a dictionary or an Internet site.

1. Name the Roman god called "Optimus, Maximus."

    _____

2. Name the state whose motto is "excelsior," a Latin adjective in the comparative degree.

    _____

3. Translate the substantive *nostrī*. Hint: Notice that *nostrī* is masculine plural, and Caesar often refers to his *mīlitēs* as *nostrī*.

    _____

4. You have learned the phrase *mea culpa* (my fault). Give the meaning of the following English words.

    culpable   _____

    exculpate   _____

    culpability   _____

    culprit   _____

IV.

Match the Latin word with its English meaning.

1.	_____ *vetus*	A.	all, every
2.	_____ *dīligēns*	B.	powerful
3.	_____ *potēns*	C.	beautiful
4.	_____ *lātus*	D.	true
5.	_____ *pulcher*	E.	old
6.	_____ *miser*	F.	poor, wretched
7.	_____ *altus*	G.	careful
8.	_____ *ferus*	H.	wide
9.	_____ *vērus*	I.	wild
10.	_____ *omnis*	J.	high, deep

V. Choose and circle the best answer from A, B, C, or D.

1. An **omnibus** volume of a poet's works will most likely contain _____ of her works.

   A. all
   B. few
   C. only the best known
   D. only the earliest examples

2. A **malediction** is a curse; what is a **benediction**?

   A. a contract
   B. a summons
   C. a prayer
   D. a blessing

3. The English words **acrimonious** and **acrid** are derived from the Latin adjective meaning

   A. diligent
   B. inveterate
   C. wild
   D. bitter

4. A person might say, "Mea culpa!" after

   A. eating dinner
   B. winning a race
   C. meeting a friend
   D. making a mistake

5. Which goddess is best known for her **pulchritude**?

   A. Juno
   B. Venus
   C. Diana
   D. Vesta

CHAPTER 24
ADVERB DERIVATIVES

Adverbs are some of the most challenging words a Latin student must master. Of course, for adverbs with English derivatives the way is smooth: make the connection between the English word and its Latin root, and you will be able to remember both easily. For example, if your teacher keeps "reiterating" a particular rule, she has repeated it again and again, and you can recall the meaning of *iterum* (again). If you have been in a hospital and heard "Stat! Stat!" over the loudspeaker, you know that a doctor is being summoned *statim* (immediately). Similarly, it is easy to link the English word "procrastinate" (put off) with the Latin word *crās* (tomorrow). Even the word for "a two-seater bicycle" that is longer than a regular bike can help you remember the Latin word *tandem* (at length). And, of course, words like *ergō* (therefore), *interim* (meanwhile), and *quondam* (formerly) are the same in both English and Latin.

Interestingly, *sīc* (thus, so) is a Latin adverb sometimes found in brackets in an English sentence when the writer wants to indicate that a quotation contains a spelling error, a grammatical mistake, curious wording, or unusual punctuation. "Sic" tells the reader that these are not the writer's own mistakes!

It can also be useful to notice that in some compound English words a Latin adverb has essentially become a prefix. For instance, the English word "peninsula" literally means "an almost island" because in Latin *paene* means "almost," and *īnsula* means "island." In the same way, *ubi* (where) is the first part of "ubiquitous" that means "everywhere."

Sometimes, a phrase, rather than a single word will help you learn the meaning of a Latin adverb. René Descartes's famous saying *cogitō ergō sum* (I think, therefore I am) makes it clear that *ergō* means "therefore." *Mox nox*, which means "Soon it will be night," is a reminder that *mox* means "soon." Mottoes like *semper parātus* (always prepared) and *semper fidēlis* (always faithful) are useful aids for remembering that *semper* means always. Even the opening words of a medieval student song, *gaudeāmus igitur* (let us rejoice therefore) is a reminder that *igitur*, like *ergō*, means "therefore."

It can be helpful to learn other synonym pairs besides *igitur* and *ergō*. For example, once you know *iterum*, you can link it with *rursus* since they both mean "again." *Statim* and *extemplō* (immediately) are another pair, as are *frūstrā* and *nēquīquam* (in vain, fruitless).

Some students also find it helpful to associate a word like *umquam* (ever) with its opposite *numquam* (never). Others connect the first letter of a Latin word like *ōlim* (once) with the English word "once," which also begins with *o*. Of course, neither of these approaches is actually dependent on English derivatives. But no matter which method you use, there will probably be a few adverbs that you simply have to write over and over, make flash cards for, or invent your own personal mnemonics!

EXERCISES

I. Fill in the blank with the meaning of each English word. Some of the English meanings were discussed above, some may require a dictionary, and some you may know already or can guess.

Latin word	English word	Meaning of English
1. *ergō* = therefore	ergo	_____
2. *iterum* = again	reiterate	_____
3. *statim* = immediately	stat.	_____
4. *ubi* = when, where	ubiquitous	_____
5. *interim* = meanwhile	interim	_____
6. *quondam* = formerly	quondam	_____
7. *frūstrā* = in vain, fruitlessly	frustrate	_____
8. *tandem* = at length	tandem (bicycle)	_____
9. *crās* = tomorrow	procrastinate	_____
10. *cōtīdiē* = daily	quotidian	_____
11. *paene* = almost	peninsula	_____
	penumbra	_____
	antepenultimate	_____
	penultimate	_____
12. *semper* = always	sempiternal	_____
13. *sīc* = so, thus	sic	_____

II. Translate.

1. cogito ergo sum _____

2. mox nox _____

3. semper paratus
   (motto of the Coast Guard) _____

4. semper fidelis
   (motto of the Marine Corps) _____

5. sic semper tyrannis
   (motto of Virginia) _____

6. gaudeamus igitur _____

III. Expand your adverb vocabulary with synonyms. If you know the meaning of the first word, you also know the synonyms. Fill in the meanings.

1. ergō, itaque, igitur _____

2. statim, extemplō _____

3. frūstrā, nēquīquam _____

4. iterum, rursus _____

IV. Give the English meaning of the opposite of each Latin word.

1. *umquam* = ever => *numquam* _____

2. *aut . . . aut* = either . . . or => *nec . . . nec* _____

V. Give the English meanings for the words below. Use a dictionary for those that you don't know.

1. saepe _____

2. diū _____

3. herī _____

4. hodiē _____

5. tamen _____

6. autem _____

7. sed _____

8. hīc _____

9. undique _____

10. nam _____

11. ōlim _____

12. nunc _____

13. iam _____

14. etiam _____

15. quoque _____

VI. Match the Latin word with its English meaning.

1. _____	*ergō*	A.	then
2. _____	*diū*	B.	at length, finally
3. _____	*paene*	C.	therefore
4. _____	*tandem*	D.	never
5. _____	*tum*	E.	for a long time
6. _____	*ōlim*	F.	almost
7. _____	*crās*	G.	yesterday
8. _____	*hodiē*	H.	today
9. _____	*herī*	I.	once
10. _____	*numquam*	J.	tomorrow

VII. Choose and circle the best answer from A, B, C, or D.

1. If an audience at a concert loved a particular singer and called out, "*Iterum!*" what does *iterum* mean?

   A. again!   B. enough!
   C. applause!   D. bow!

2. The saying "tempus fugit" is similar in meaning to

   A. *semper fidēlis*   B. *mox nox*
   C. *post mortem*   D. *mīrābile dictū*

3. Where would you most likely hear a loudspeaker broadcasting the word "stat"?

   A. a theater   B. a restaurant
   C. a hospital   D. a shopping mall

4. A Roman mother might begin a story to her children about a long-ago adventure with the word

   A. *crās*   B. *hodiē*
   C. *paene*   D. *ōlim*

5. If a Roman army camp is assaulted *undique*, the enemy is attacking

   A. from the rear   B. on the left
   C. on all sides   D. near the gate

CHAPTER 25
LOOK-ALIKE DERIVATIVES

Elementary school students learning to read and spell are often irritated by English homonyms like "to," "too," "two" or "they're," "there," and "their." And older students taking Latin frequently find sound-alike or look-alike words similarly challenging. Luckily, a tried and true way to conquer these troublesome Latin words is to associate each one with an English derivative. If, for example, you remember that the English word "premonition" means "a warning," you can easily remember that *moneō* in Latin means "warn, advise." Furthermore, you will not confuse *moneō* with *maneō* (stay, remain) if you know that *maneō* is the root of the English word "permanent." You will not mistake the Latin word for book, *liber, librī* (m.) with *liber, lībera, līberum*, the Latin word for "free," when you think of the English derivatives "library" and "liberty." Of course, you will not mix up either *liber, librī* (m.) or *liber, lībera, līberum* with the Latin word *lībra, -ae* (f.) (pound) because you are familiar with the abbreviation lb. on bags of flour, sugar, or potatoes. If you go to England, you will also see the symbol £, derived from the capital letter *L*, as an abbreviation for a pound coin.

Sometimes a helpful derivative is actually made up of Latin words. For example, *bellum* is the Latin word for "war," and *ante* means "before." Thus, "antebellum" means "before the war" and refers to the period in American history before the Civil War. Other derivatives such as "belligerent" (warlike) and "bellicose" (aggressive) will help you remember that the neuter noun *bellum* is different from the adjective *bellus, -a, -um* (beautiful).

Sometimes, the connection between a Latin word and its English derivative is a little hard to see at first glance. For example, you may have easily learned to connect the English word "vital" with the Latin *vīta* (life), but you are having trouble with *vitium* (crime, vice). Here, the English word "vicious" (cruel, spiteful) does not appear to have any connection with the Latin word *vitium* unless you recognize that the *–ti* in *vitium* has become the *–ci* in "vicious." Similarly, you might wonder how *iaceō* (to lie, be situated) relates to "adjacent" (lying next to). This time, you need to remember that the Latin alphabet did not include the letter *j* but used the letter *i* as both a vowel and a consonant.

Finally, an English derivative can sometimes help you master a particularly challenging Latin word like the irregular noun *vīs* (force, violence). While it is easy to confuse *vīs* with *vir* (man), knowing the English words "vim" (vigor or energy) and "virile" (having the characteristics of a man) will help you keep the meanings of *vīs* and *vir* straight.

The list of Latin words that look and sound alike included below in exercise I is quite long, but associating each Latin word with a familiar English word is the key to mastering these important vocabulary words.

EXERCISES

I. Fill in the blank with the meaning of each English word. Some of the English meanings were discussed above, some may require a dictionary, and some you may know already or can guess.

	Latin word	*English word*	*Meaning of English*
1.	*maneō, -ēre, mānsī, mānsum* = stay, remain	permanent	
2.	*moneō, -ēre, monuī, monitum* = warn	premonition	
3.	*bellum, -ī* (n.) = war	belligerent	
		antebellum	
		bellicose	
4.	*bellus, -a, -um* = beautiful	belle	
5.	*pār, paris* = equal	parity	
6.	*pars, partis* (f.) = part	part	
7.	*mora, -ae* (f.) = delay	moratorium	
8.	*mors, mortis* (f.) = death	mortal	
9.	*liber, librī* (m.) = book	library	
10.	*lībra, -ae* (f.) = weight, pound	lb.	
11.	*līber, lībera, līberum* = free	liberty	
12.	*vīta, -ae* (f.) = life	vital	
13.	*vitium, -ī* (n.) = vice, crime	vicious	
14.	*vītō* (1) = avoid	inevitable	
15.	*audeō, -ēre, ausus* = dare	audacious	
16.	*audiō, -īre, -īvī, -ītum* = hear, listen	audio	
17.	*servō* (1) = keep, guard, save	conservation	
18.	*serviō, -īre, -īvī, -ītum* = be a slave to, serve	servile	
19.	*iaceō, iacēre, iacuī, iacitum* = lie, be situated	adjacent	

20. *iaciō, iacere, iēcī, iactum*   eject   _____
    = throw

21. *vīs, vīs* (f.) = force, violence   vim   _____

22. *vir, virī* (m.) = man   virile   _____

23. *putō* (1) = think   compute   _____

24. *pōnō, -ere, posuī, positum*   exponent   _____
    = put, place

II. Translate.

1. ex libris   _____

2. post mortem   _____

III. Match the Latin word with its English meaning.

1. _____ *serviō*   A. equal

2. _____ *moneō*   B. stay, remain

3. _____ *bellus, -a, -um*   C. dare

4. _____ *iaciō*   D. life

5. _____ *mora*   E. man

6. _____ *audeō*   F. beautiful

7. _____ *pār, paris*   G. throw

8. _____ *vīta*   H. warn, advise

9. _____ *maneō*   I. delay

10. _____ *vir*   J. serve, be a slave to

IV. Answer by giving the meaning of each Latin word.

1. The English word "premonition" means a warning. What does the Latin verb *moneō* mean?

    _____

2. The English word "belligerent" means warlike. What does the Latin noun *bellum* mean?

    _____

3. The English word "parity" comes from the Latin adjective *pār*. What does *pār* mean?

    _____

4. The English word "liberty" comes from the Latin adjective *līber, lībera, līberum*. What does *līber, lībera, līberum* mean?

    _____

    What is the Latin word for "children"?

    _____

5. The English words "conservation" and "preservation" come from the Latin verb *servō*. What does *servō* mean?

    _____

6. The English words "edict" and "diction" come from the Latin verb *dīcō*. What does *dīcō* mean?

    _____

7. The English word "exponent" comes from the Latin verb *pōnō*. What does *pōnō* mean?

    _____

8. The English word "compute" comes from the Latin verb *putō*. What does *putō* mean?

    _____

9. The English word "vim" is the accusative of the Latin word *vīs*. What does *vīs* mean?

    _____

10. The English word "adjacent" comes from the Latin preposition *ad* plus the Latin verb *iaceō*. What does *iaceō* mean?

    _____

V. Choose and circle the best answer from A, B, C, or D.

1. Based on its Latin root, what is the meaning of the English word **admonish**?

    A. warn   B. pretend
    C. advertise   D. return

2. The **belligerent** behavior of the country's former ally was surprising.

    A. secretive   B. aggressive
    C. long term   D. inconsistent

3. The English words **parity** and **disparity** come from the Latin word that means

    A. final
    B. distinguished
    C. equal
    D. limited

4. When I buy a new book, I always put my name on a bookplate with the words *Ex Libris*. This phrase shows

    A. the book's owner
    B. the book's weight
    C. the book's price
    D. the book's author

5. The English words **computer**, **reputation**, and **amputate** are derived from the Latin verb

    A. *possum*
    B. *pōnō*
    C. *pellō*
    D. *putō*

6. The English word **vim** is a derivative of the Latin word

    A. *vīs*
    B. *vir*
    C. *vīrus*
    D. *vicis*

APPENDIX A

ENGLISH DERIVATIVE LISTS BY CHAPTER

NB: The bolded words are those defined in the chapter essay or presented in exercise I, while the other words are from the other exercises.

PART I: AFFIXES

CHAPTER 1: SUFFIXES

Verb:

−esce

−fy

−ate

Noun:

−ance, −ence

−ary, −arium

−ation, −tion

−el, −il, −ol, −ule

−ment

−ndum, −nda, −nd

−tor, −trix

−ure

Adjective:

−able, −ible

−al, −an, −ian, −ar, −ary

−ate, −ent

−ine, −ile

−ose

Greek:

−graphy

−logy

CHAPTER 2: PREPOSITION AND PREFIX DERIVATIVES

a−, ab−

ad−

ante−

circum−

contra−

cum−, con−, com−, co−

de−

e−, ex−

in−

infra−

inter−

ob−

post−

per−

preter−

pro−

re−

sine−

sub−

super−

trans−

ultra−

PART II: SPECIAL TOPIC DERIVATIVES
CHAPTER 3: ANIMAL DERIVATIVES

aggregate
animal
animation
apiarist
apiary
aquiline
asinine
avian
aviary
aviation
aviator
bovine
canine
capricious

Capricorn
columbarium
congregate
congregation
egregious
feline
inanimate
Leo
leonine
lupine
murine
muscle
ovine
passerine

pastor
pastoral
porcine
segregate
sibilant
simian
strident
taurine
Taurus
ululation
ursine
vaccination
vaccine
vulpine

CHAPTER 4: COLOR DERIVATIVES

Ag
albino
Alba Longa
Albion
Argentina
Au

candid
candidate
cerulean
corpus luteum
denigrate
fulvous

obfuscate
porphyry
rubicund
rubric
viridian

CHAPTER 5: MONEY DERIVATIVES

Au
bursar
bursary
capital
confiscate
copious
credit
d.
debase
decrease

devalue
diversion
Fe
fiscal
impecunious
inflation
invert
lucrative
marsupial
money

numismatics
obverse
Pb
pecuniary
plutocrat
reimburse
remuneration
reverse

CHAPTER 6: NUMBER DERIVATIVES

cardinal	**November**	**quintuplets**
centennial	**novena**	**secondary**
centimeter	**octagon**	**September**
centipede	octane	**septuagenarian**
December	**October**	sextant
decimeter	octogenarian	**sextuplets**
duet	ordinal	**tertiary**
duo	**prime**	**trefoil**
hectare	**quadrangle**	**triad**
kilometer	quadrennial	triumvirate
meter	**quadruped**	unicorn
milligram	**quart**	uniform
millimeter	quincunx	**unify**
millipede	**quintet**	unite

CHAPTER 7: BODY PARTS DERIVATIVES

accord	digit	**patella**
alveoli	**digital**	**pectoral**
atrium	**dorsal**	pedagogue
aural	endorse	**pedestal**
capillary	**expectorate**	pedestrian
capital	**fibula**	pediatrician
capitol	**genuflect**	**plantar**
cerebral	**humerus**	podiatry
cerebrum	**lateral**	prestidigitation
cochlea	latitude	**sanguinary**
cochlear	**manual**	sanguine
concord	manufacture	**sinus**
cordial	manuscript	**supercilious**
corporal	**oculist**	tibia
corpulent	**oral**	ulna
decapitate	**ossify**	**ventral**

CHAPTER 8: POLITICAL DERIVATIVES

ambition	lectern	**Republican**
ballot	**legal**	sedate
candidate	legend	sedentary
citizen	legible	**senate**
conservative	**liberal**	**senator**
Democrat	**liberty**	senescent
election	**mandate**	senile
eradicate	**president**	**suffrage**
fascism	radical	tribune
gubernatorial	**referendum**	**veto**
inaugurate	**republic**	**vote**

CHAPTER 9: TIME DERIVATIVES

aet.	**equinox**	**millennial**
annual	**estivate**	**November**
Ante Meridiem	**febrile**	**October**
April	**February**	**perennial**
August	**hibernate**	**Post Meridiem**
autumnal	**hibernation**	**secular**
biennial	**horology**	**sempiternal**
calendar	**January**	**September**
centennial	**July**	**solstice**
circadian	**June**	**vernal**
contemporary	**March**	**vigilant**
December	**May**	**vigilante**
diary	**mensal**	

CHAPTER 10: MYTHOLOGY DERIVATIVES

aegis	iridescent	**mercury**
ambrosia	**jovial**	**nectar**
aphrodisiac	**Junoesque**	**pantheon**
caduceus	**lethal**	**stygian**
cereal	**lethargic**	trident
cornucopia	**lyric**	**venereal**
cupidity	**martial**	**volcano**
erotic	**mercurial**	**vulcanize**

CHAPTER 11: SCHOOL AND BOOK DERIVATIVES

abacus	incunabulum	**penmanship**
arena	interlude	**postlude**
calculus	**library**	prelude
capsule	manuscript	**scribe**
chart	**membrane**	**stylus**
codicil	**palimpsest**	**tablet**
cursive	**paper**	**title**
disciple	**papyrology**	**umbilical**
discipline	pedagogical	**voluminous**
education	**pedagogy**	

CHAPTER 12: GEOGRAPHICAL DERIVATIVES

Africa	**flume**	**orb**
Asia	**geography**	**orient**
atlas	**insular**	**oriental**
aurora borealis	**insulate**	**patriotic**
Australia	latitude	**pelagic**
cartographer	longitude	peninsula
cartography	**map**	prime meridian
continent	**marine**	**provincial**
Corsica	**Mediterranean**	**repatriate**
derivative	**meridian**	Sardinia
estuary	**mile**	**terrain**
Europe	**mundane**	**transcontinental**
expatriate	**occidental**	**trivia**
extraterrestrial	ocean	**zephyr**

CHAPTER 13: HALLOWEEN DERIVATIVES

adumbrate	**lapidary**	**sepulcher**
concatenation	**larva**	tibia
delectable	larval	ulna
dilapidated	**ossify**	**umbrage**
exhume	patella	**umbrella**
fraudulent	**penumbra**	**vinculum**
impersonate	**posthumous**	
inhume	pupa	

CHAPTER 14: THANKSGIVING DERIVATIVES

aqueduct
carnivore
comestible
commensal
companion
cornucopia
crust
culinary
dulcimer

edible
grace
gratitude
herbivore
incarnation
ingrate
melody
omelet
omnivore

oval
petroleum
piscatorial
postprandial
recipe
scissors
viaduct
wine

PART III: GRAMMAR-RELATED DERIVATIVES

CHAPTER 15: FIRST AND SECOND DECLENSION MASCULINE AND FEMININE NOUN DERIVATIVES

abundant
agriculture
amiable
amicable
ancillary
annunciation
aqua vitae
aquaculture
aquamarine
aquarium
aquatic
aqueduct
aquifer
defamation
deification
deify
deity

deviate
enunciate
enunciation
epistle
expatriate
extraterrestrial
feminine
insular
legate
nautical
patriot
peninsula
Pennsylvania
poet
poetic
pronunciation
puerile

redundant
repatriate
Spotsylvania
sylvan
terra cotta
terrace
terrain
terrarium
terrestrial
Transylvania
trivia
undulation
via
viaduct
virile
vital

CHAPTER 16: SECOND DECLENSION NEUTER NOUN DERIVATIVES

antebellum	datum, data	**premium**
auxiliary	**donate**	regal
bellicose	**edification**	sepulcher
belligerent	**edifice**	signal
celestial	**frumenty**	tablet
consul	medium, media	**verb**
council	**odious**	**verbal**
counsel	**otiose**	verbose
cubicle	peril	**viniferous**

CHAPTER 17: THIRD DECLENSION MASCULINE AND FEMININE NOUN DERIVATIVES

accelerate	infanticide	**regal**
advocate	**laborious**	**regicide**
amorous	**liberty**	**sorority**
city	**matriarch**	suicide
civic	matriarchal	**timorous**
crucial	matricide	tyrannicide
crux	**mores**	**urban**
cupidity	**nepotism**	**urbane**
deprecate	**pacify**	**uxorious**
elaborate	**paternal**	**verity**
equivocal	patriarchal	**virtue**
fratricide	patricide	**virtuoso**
homage	pesticide	
homicide	**precarious**	

CHAPTER 18: THIRD DECLENSION NEUTER NOUN DERIVATIVES

capital	**invulnerable**	**onus**
capitol	**itinerary**	Op.
corporal	**luminary**	**opus**
decapitate	**luminous**	**pectoral**
expectorate	**multilateral**	pro tem.
federation	**nominal**	**remunerate**
flume	**nominate**	**subliminal**
fulminate	**nominative**	**temporary**
genus	**numinous**	**unilateral**
illuminate	**onerous**	**vulnerable**

CHAPTER 19: PRONOUN DERIVATIVES

ad hoc	et alii, et alia	quid pro quo
alias	id	quiddity
alibi	id est	quidnunc
ego	me	quorum
egotism	pax nobiscum	semper eadem
egotistical	pax vobiscum	vade mecum

CHAPTER 20: FIRST AND SECOND CONJUGATION VERB DERIVATIVES

adjutant	deride	premonition
admonish	erratum, errata	prepare
advocate	error	preserve
amateur	habitat	provoke
ambulatory	ignoramus	pugilist
amity	imperative	pugnacious
caret	insuperable	repugnant
caveat	invulnerable	servile
conjugation	laud	status
conserve	laudable	tenet
dative	monitor	visible
datum, data	observe	vocation
debt	permanent	vocative
delete	placebo	

CHAPTER 21: THIRD AND FOURTH CONJUGATION AND IRREGULAR VERB DERIVATIVES

actor	credit	insurrection
agenda	deposit	nolo contendere
agent	derelict	petition
appetite	dictate	position
audible	essence	posse
audition	exit	potential
benevolent	exponent	proceed
captivate	extol	procession
captive	factory	proponent
captor	fraction	refer
centripetal	frangible	regal
compete	futuristic	relate

relict
relinquish
reliquary
revolution
revolve
secede
secession

sensitive
sentient
tactful
tactile
tangent
transfer
transient

transit
translate
translation
volition
volume

CHAPTER 22: DEPONENT VERB DERIVATIVES

affable
arbitration
arbitrator
cohort
colloquial
colloquium
consecutive
consequence
deponent
elapse

elocution
eloquent
exhort
ineffable
infant
loquacious
monologue
moratorium
mortuary
neonatal

passion
patient
prenatal
Renaissance/Renascence
reverence
sequel
sequence
soliloquy
usury

CHAPTER 23: ADJECTIVE DERIVATIVES

*Positive Degree Adjective
  Derivatives*
accelerate
acrid
acrimonious
altitude
alto
belle
benediction
bonus
clarify
commiserate
culpability
culpable
culprit
diligent
embellish

equity
exalt
exculpate
facility
feral
fortitude
ingent
inveterate
latitude
liberty
magnitude
malediction
multitude
nullify
omnibus
omnipotent
omniscient

pulchritude
simile
verify
verisimilitude
veteran

*Comparative and Superlative
  Degree Adjective Derivatives*
ameliorate
major
maximum
minor
minimum
minus
optimist
pejorative
pessimist

CHAPTER 24: ADVERB DERIVATIVES

antepenultimate	penumbra	sic
ergo	procrastinate	stat.
frustrate	quondam	tandem (bicycle)
interim	quotidian	ubiquitous
peninsula	reiterate	
penultimate	sempiternal	

CHAPTER 25: LOOK-ALIKE DERIVATIVES

adjacent	diction	part
admonish	disparity	permanent
amputate	edict	premonition
antebellum	eject	preservation
audacious	exponent	reputation
audio	inevitable	servile
belle	lb.	vicious
bellicose	liberty	vim
belligerent	library	virile
compute	moratorium	vital
computer	mortal	
conservation	parity	

APPENDIX B
LATIN PHRASES USED IN ENGLISH

ab ovo usque ad mala

ad hoc

ad hominem

ad nauseam

alter ego

amicus curiae

anno domini (A.D.)

ante meridiem (A.M.)

ante bellum

ars longa, vita brevis

carpe diem

civis Romanus sum

cogito ergo sum

cornucopia

corpus delicti

cum grano salis

cum laude

de gustibus non est disputandum

dies irae

docendo discitur

dona nobis pacem

dramatis personae

dulce et decorum est pro patria mori

e pluribus unum

errare humanum est

et alia, et alii (et al.)

excelsior (motto of New York)

exeunt omnes

ex libris

ex tempore

gaudeamus igitur

habeas corpus

homo sapiens

id est (i.e)

in hoc signo vinces

in vino veritas

labor omnia vincit

lapsus linguae

lapsus memoriae

lapsus pennae

magnum opus

mea culpa

memento mori

morituri te salutamus

mox nox

nolens, volens

noli me tangere!

non sequitur

numen lumen (motto of the University of Wisconsin)

onus probandi

Pater Noster

pax nobiscum

pax vobiscum

Pax Romana

per capita

per centum

per diem

persona non grata

post hoc ergo propter hoc

post meridiem (P.M.)

post mortem

post scriptum (P.S.)

pro tempore

quid pro quo

rara avis

requiescat in pace (R.I.P.)

res ipsa loquitur

semper eadem

semper fidelis (motto of the Marine Corps)

semper paratus (motto of the Coast Guard)

sic transit gloria mundi

sic semper tyrannis (motto of Virginia)

sine die

sine qua non

statim (stat.)

status quo

status quo ante

sub poena

sui generis

tempus fugit

terra firma

terra incognita

urbs aeterna

vade mecum

verbum sapientibus satis est

videre est credere

veni, vidi, vici

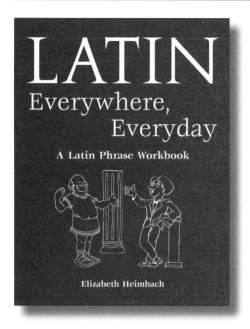

Latin Everywhere, Everyday

Elizabeth Heimbach, CD by James Chochola

Student Text: viii + 152 pp. (2004) 8½" x 11" Paperback
ISBN 978-0-86516-572-4

Teacher's Guide: iv + 164 pp. + CD-ROM (2005) 8½" x 11" Paperback
ISBN 978-0-86516-589-2

Latin Everywhere, Everyday is a source beyond compare for middle school and high school students. Well-known Latin phrases are accompanied by English words derived from these phrases, historical facts, and explanations pertinent to the words.

Features:

- One Latin phrase for every day of the school year with five on a page so that a week's work can be viewed at one time
- A reservoir of explanations, examples, translations, and accompanying exercises
- An abundance of derivatives that flows through the explanations of the phrases
- A profusion of Latin abbreviations and mottoes
- A steady stream of projects and games to keep students engaged in the learning process
- A source of unique historical facts and of the ubiquity of Latin in our everyday lives

The student workbook is designed for students who want to learn Latin phrases, abbreviations, and mottoes and how to use them correctly in English. This practical volume can also serve as an effective introduction to Latin.

The teacher's manual contains the answers to all the exercises in the student workbook along with additional exercises and answers for those who have studied Latin. Some additional games and projects are also included in the teacher's manual. The accompanying CD, by James Chochola, offers a clear Latin pronunciation of each phrase, motto, and abbreviation.

BOLCHAZY-CARDUCCI PUBLISHERS, INC.
WWW.BOLCHAZY.COM

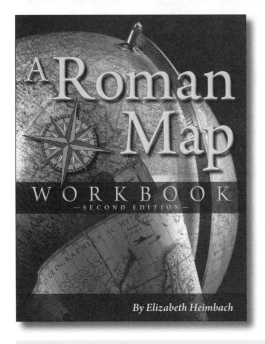

A Roman Map
WORKBOOK
—SECOND EDITION—

by Elizabeth Heimbach

Student Text: vii + 140 pp., 20 maps (2013) 8½" x 11" Paperback, ISBN 978-0-86516-799-5
Teacher's Guide: vii + 86 pp. (2013) 6" x 9" Paperback, ISBN 978-0-86516-762-9

A Roman Map Workbook introduces students to the geography of Rome and the Roman world. Veteran high school and college Latin teacher Elizabeth Heimbach provides students, especially those studying Latin, with a thorough grounding in the geography of the Roman world. The workbook walks students through each map, making connections to Roman history and literature. The maps complement subjects and periods covered in the Latin and ancient history classroom.

The Second Edition includes minor changes to the Roman World, Conquest of Italy, Punic Wars, and Pompeii maps. This edition also includes a copy of the Pompeii city plan without building names. The Roman Forum plan has been significantly expanded to include the Arch of Titus and buildings in its vicinity. The map of the Roman Empire under Trajan includes both the boundaries and names of the Roman provinces. Additions have made to some exercises, especially those accompanying the Roman Forum and the Roman Empire under Trajan.

Features:
- Maps: Ancient Italy, The Roman World, Roman Roads of Italy, Roads of Roman Empire, City of Rome: Seven Hills Schematic, City of Rome: Districts and Landmarks, City of Rome: Forum Romanum, Bay of Naples, City of Pompeii, Roman History: Conquest of Italy, Roman History: Punic Wars, Roman History: Roman Empire under Trajan, Ancient Greece, City of Athens, Gaul, Roman Britain, "Journey of Odysseus," "Journey of Aeneas," Ancient Latin Writers, Later Latin Writers
- Narrative explication for each map, noting the historical and literary significance of place-names
- Map-based activities and exercises, including work with blank maps
- Three sets of Certamen questions

BOLCHAZY-CARDUCCI PUBLISHERS, INC.
www.BOLCHAZY.com

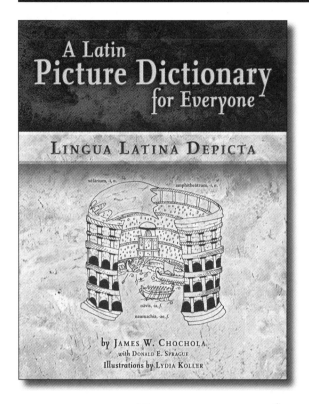

A Latin Picture Dictionary for Everyone
Lingua Latina Depicta

JAMES CHOCHOLA
with Donald E. Sprague
Illustrations by Lydia Koller

Student Text: viii + 205 pp. (2017) 8½" x 11" Paperback
ISBN 978-0-86516-749-0

Teacher's Guide: (2017) 8½" x 11" Paperback
ISBN 978-0-86516-855-8

Everyone can learn some Latin visually!

Designed for Latin students, *A Latin Picture Dictionary for Everyone* asks the learner to make a ready connection between an image and its corresponding Latin word. Illustrated exercises provide an opportunity for students to practice with and internalize the Latin vocabulary.

Features

- Black-and-white line drawings present everyday objects and scenes from everyday life—animals and numbers, colors, the family, buildings, transportation, the house, furniture, pastimes, professions, the military, parts of the body, clothing, food shopping, food preparation, and the arts—one image from the Roman world and a corresponding image from the modern world. The line drawings invite students to color the pictures.

- Each object is drawn for ready recognition and easy connection to its Latin label.

- A set of exercises, of varied complexity, accompanies each set of illustrations.

- Appendices include Pronunciation of Classical Latin, Major Parts of Speech and Their Uses, How Latin Words Work: Nouns, Verbs, Adjectives, A Grammatical Outline

- A Pictorial Glossary of Additional Latin Vocabulary and Synonyms

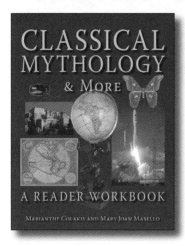

Classical Mythology and More
A Reader Workbook

Marianthe Colakis and Mary Joan Masello

Student Text: xii + 460 pp., 519 illustrations & 6 maps (2007)
8½" x 11" Paperback, ISBN 978-0-86516-573-1
Teacher's Guide: 36 pp. (2008) 8½" x 11" Paperback, ISBN 978-0-86516-747-6

This engaging workbook is an unparalleled classical mythology resource for middle- and high-school aged students. Students in Latin, English, and Language Arts classes will enjoy and learn from these fresh retellings of timeless tales from Hesiod, Homer, Ovid, and other ancient authors. A wide variety of exercises, reflections, and vocabulary enrichment tasks accompany each myth. Creation myths, stories of the Olympians and Titans, legends of the Trojan War cycle, love stories, and tales of transformation are all included here. Numerous illustrations and a wide variety of exercises, reflections, and vocabulary enrichment tasks accompany each myth chapter. Students preparing for the ACL Medusa Myth Exam and the ACL National Mythology Exam will find in this an indispensable tool.

Features • Fresh retellings of favorite myths, based on primary Latin and Greek sources • Numerous illustrations that show myth's influence on art, science, and popular culture • Maps illustrating routes of heroes and key locations • Sidebar summaries that keep the reader oriented and engaged • Varied exercises at the end of each chapter • Quirky and fun information about English words derived from the myths • Reflections upon the enduring quality and influence of the myths • Glossary of names and places, arranged chapter by chapter for quick review

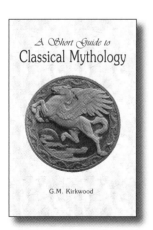

A Short Guide to Classical Mythology

G. M. Kirkwood

120 pp. (1959, reprint 2003) 6" x 9" Paperback, ISBN 978-0-86516-309-6

A Short Guide to Classical Mythology is a concise reference for general readers, students, and teachers. Kirkwood's treatment of the characters, settings, and stories of ancient mythology emphasizes their importance in Western literature. The entries are ordered alphabetically and vary in length according to their significance.

Features • Complete reference list with pronunciations • Principal stories of classical mythology • Emphasis on literary importance of Greek myths

 BOLCHAZY-CARDUCCI PUBLISHERS, INC.
WWW.BOLCHAZY.COM

FOLLOW YOUR FATES SERIES

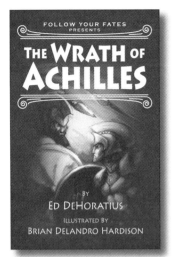

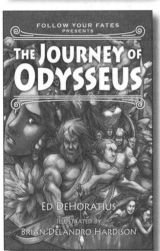

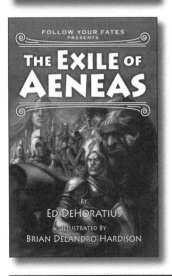

Ed DeHoratius's three dramatic action adventures let YOU experience firsthand the wrenching decisions of the ancient Mediterranean world's most illustrious heroes:

In *The Wrath of Achilles*, you are Achilles, the greatest hero of ancient Greece. On Troy's battlefields will you honor your code and not fight, or stand beside your men?

x + 62 pp. (2009) 5" x 7¾" Paperback, ISBN 978-0-86516-708-7

In *The Journey of Odysseus*, you are Odysseus, the wiliest hero of ancient Greece. Your love of family is as strong as your quest for adventure. What will you do, when given the choice of immortality, or when trapped in a cave by a man-eating monster?

x + 118 pp. (2009) 5" x 7¾" Paperback, ISBN 978-0-86516-710-0

In *The Exile of Aeneas*, you are Aeneas, Troy's preeminent hero. Your integrity is legendary, but can it withstand your city's destruction, grueling exile, and another war?

x + 114 pp. (2010) 5" x 7¾" Paperback, ISBN 978-0-86516-709-4

Features of each *Follow Your Fates* adventure:

- Prose story that thrusts you the reader right into the action
- Multiple different endings—depending on your choices
- Illustrations by award-winning comic book artist Brian Delandro Hardison
- Glossary of names, with pronunciation guide
- Series website: www.bolchazy.com/followyourfates

BOLCHAZY-CARDUCCI PUBLISHERS, INC.
WWW.BOLCHAZY.COM